BRIDGE
FOR EVERYONE

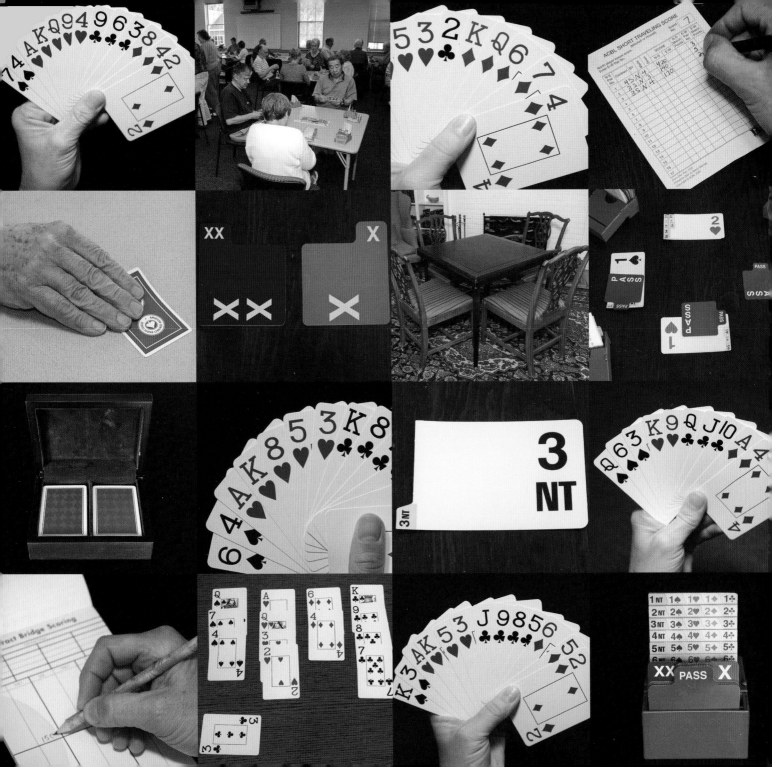

KNACK

BRIDGE
FOR EVERYONE

A Step-by-Step Guide to Rules, Bidding, and Play of the Hand

D. W. CRISFIELD

Photographs by Stephen Gorman and Eli Burakian

Guilford, Connecticut
An imprint of Globe Pequot Press

Editor-in-Chief: Maureen Graney
Editor: Katie Benoit
Cover Design: Paul Beatrice, Bret Kerr
Text Design: Paul Beatrice
Layout: Maggie Peterson
Cover photos by Stephen Gorman and Eli Burakian
Interior photos by Stephen Gorman and Eli Burakian

Library of Congress Cataloging-in-Publication Data
Crisfield, Deborah.
 Knack bridge for everyone : a step-by-step guide to rules, bidding, and play of the hand / D.W. Crisfield ; photographs by Stephen Gorman and Eli Burakian.
     p. cm.
 Includes index.
 ISBN 978-1-59921-615-7
 1. Contract bridge. I. Title.
 GV1282.3.C754 2010
 795.41'5—dc22
                    2009032200

Printed in China

10 9 8 7 6 5 4 3 2 1

Dedication

To my first bridge teachers—Mom, Nana, and Grandma—who taught me the game because apparently I'd be lost at college if I didn't know how to play (they were completely wrong about that).

Acknowledgments

I first want to thank my husband for encouraging me to write this book and my two children for being tolerant of a mother who spent the early part of 2009 facing a computer screen.

Second, I couldn't possibly write a bridge book without acknowledging my favorite Swiss Team, regular partners, and early students: Jennifer Feltes, Karen Haines, and Jane Grewcock. In a perfect world, this would be another dedication, but I have to thank them not only for being the guinea pigs on whom I honed my teaching skills but also for being good friends, great bridge players, and hugely entertaining traveling companions. Jennifer also gets a big shout out for holding hundreds of hands of cards for the photos in this book.

Moving on to other people in the bridge world who I owe various debts to: Thanks to all my students (way too many to name, but almost without exception really nice fun people); to Cyndi Sauvage for being my first regular partner, introducing me to the world of tournament bridge, and helping me get my first mastepoints; to Marilyn Millard for taking me from Goren bidding to Standard American; to Ingrid Roden for being a great partner and my most accomplished student (so far!); and to Peter Jones for elevating my game to another level.

I'd also like to thank my hand models (and bridge students), Helene Hulse and Laurie Gerard. And finally, thanks to Eli Burakian—a very fun and accommodating photographer—and editors Michelle Stevens-Orton, Maureen Graney and Katie Benoit.

Photographer Acknowledgments

The photographers would like to thank Thomas Kurtz, Agnes Kurtz, and Jesse Stalker for their help with the book photography.

CONTENTS

INTRODUCTION— DON'T SKIP THIS PART!

Sometimes when I read a book, I skip the introduction and go right into the meat of the book, but I encourage you to spend a minute or two with me while I explain both the game of bridge and my approach to it in this book.

First let me say that while this book is designed to introduce a brand new player to the wonderful game of bridge, this book is also loaded with instruction that will be helpful for players who already have a rudimentary knowledge of the game and will offer the beginning player years of extra knowledge.

Bridge is a complex card game. Its origins can be found in much older games, but bridge really became the game

it is today in the 1920s. Because the game offers continuous challenges, even to the experts who rule the game, it caught on quickly, spread like crazy, and became a national pastime. But this is a "How To" book, not a history book, so let's get down to the actual details of how the game is played.

Most explanations of a game begin with the "object of the game," but bridge is so complicated that it's hard to describe the object of the game until you know some aspects of the game. Still, pared down to its barest bones, you could say the object of bridge is to score higher than your opponents, or to take more tricks. But at this point, besides oversimplifying a complicated game, this information won't get you started playing and ends up being more confusing than helpful.

So I beg you to stick with this book from start to finish and to get comfortable with the fact that the object of the game will unfold as the game unfolds. Ultimately, you will be rewarded for enduring the process. You will grasp the goals of bidding, playing, defending, and scoring and how each hand involves all four aspects, and you will understand how they all relate to the ultimate goal of winning bridge. You'll be hooked on the most challenging card game ever invented.

I've written this book to be read consecutively, but you absolutely do not have to follow that to the letter. For instance, you can skim over the equipment parts in Chapter 1 if that doesn't interest you—although every other piece of Chapter 1 is essential. And in the scoring chapter, I explain several different types of scoring. As long as you read about the basics of scoring, you can return to the varieties of scoring later.

I guarantee you will feel overwhelmed. But persevere. For example, the chapter on scoring is placed second because the bidding makes no sense if you don't understand the scoring. On the other hand, the scoring is one of the most complicated parts of playing the game. So get a feel for it, but don't worry too much about grasping it fully right away.

In this book, I begin with the bidding, because every hand starts with an auction. However, in my classes, I teach the play first, because it's hard for players to know why they're bidding if they haven't played a hand yet. If that works better for you, feel free to skip ahead to the chapter on playing, returning to the bidding chapter a little later.

Finally, I want to tell you to practice, practice, practice. Deal out hands when you're by yourself. Get a bridge computer game that will deal them for you. Find three friends and just play. The game is the world's best teacher, and if you're a card fan, then you'll quickly discover that bridge is the world's best card game.

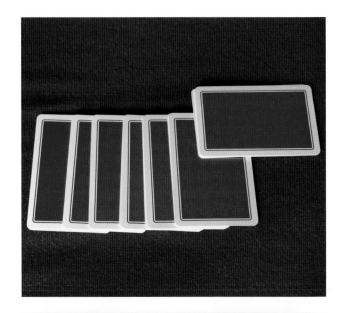

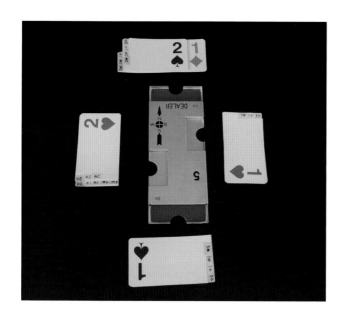

EQUIPMENT
Everything you need to begin playing the game of bridge

Bridge is a card game, so you'll need a deck of cards. In fact, as long as you have cards and three other people, you can play the game. Everything else can be accommodated.

But even though cards are the only absolute requirement, bridge does come with a few other needs. It's a game that's usually played around a square card table, one player on each side. Bridge is a partnership game, so the player sitting across from you at the table is your partner. The other two players are your opponents.

Presumably when you play bridge, you'll want to keep score, and like everything else in bridge, the score sheet is complicated. If you're playing rubber bridge, you'll want a score sheet that is divided into columns, with a line crossing the middle of it. If you're playing duplicate bridge, the score sheet travels

Playing Cards

- A package of bridge cards always has two decks.

- Since the entire deck is dealt each time, it's more efficient to have one person shuffling while another is dealing.

- Bridge cards are about $1/8$ of an inch thinner than poker cards to make it easier to hold 13 cards in your hand at once.

- Aces are considered the high cards. Twos are at the bottom.

The Venue

- Bridge is usually played at a card table or a square game table.

- The table can be folding or permanent.

- There should be one chair on each side of the table.

with the duplicate board. If you're playing social bridge, then you'll want a bridge tally, something that each individual player carries with her as she plays with different partners.

Now you have to pick your venue. If you're starting your bridge career at a bridge club, you'll probably jump right into duplicate bridge. In this case then, you'll be using duplicate boards and bidding boxes. If, however, you begin by playing bridge in the home, you won't need any more equipment than what I've already described.

Duplicate Boards

- Duplicate boards are metal or plastic devices used to keep the individual hands in a deal separate.

- Each board has four slots, each able to hold 13 cards and marked with North, South, East, and West.

- During the play, the players keep their cards in front of them. At the end, they return their 13 cards to the slot in front of them.

- The board is then passed to another table to play.

Bidding Boxes

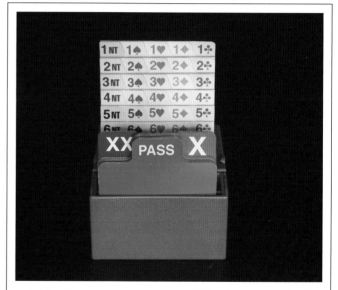

- Bidding boxes are generally small plastic boxes that hold every single legal bridge bid.

- The players use these boxes so that the bids are visual rather than verbal.

- Bidding boxes were developed to remove the effect of voice inflection from bidding, but most players have come to appreciate the advantages of seeing the bidding, rather than just hearing it.

DEAL OUT THE DECK
It's best to learn as you go, so deal the cards and jump right in

To start a bridge game, one entire deck is dealt out to the four players. There are 52 cards in the deck, so that means that each player gets 13 cards. For now, we'll say that the object of the game is to use your set of 13 cards in the most productive way possible.

So let's jump in. Players each look at their own hand, but they must keep it hidden from the other three players. As soon as you get your cards, you should sort them into suits.

Each hand begins with bidding—also called the auction—which is a method of describing your hand to your partner while competing with your opponents to choose the trump suit. (For those of you who haven't played a card game with a trump suit, it will be explained shortly.)

In an actual auction, bidders have a sense of how much

Sorting Your Hand

- Most players find it helpful to sort numerically within the suit.

- Many people seem to prefer to alternate red and black in order to visually keep the suits separate.

- Others prefer to sort the suits in order of the suits rankings: spades, hearts, diamonds, clubs.

Counting Your Points

- Let's count the points in this hand.

- There is one ace. That's 4 points.

- Add that to two kings, each worth 3 points: 4+3+3.

- Now add the one jack: 4+3+3+1. This hand is valued at 11 points.

money they want to spend on an item, which tells them how high they should bid. In a bridge auction, you don't have money, but you use the value of the cards in your hand to give yourself some idea of how high you should go in the bidding. Most people use a 4 point evaluation system: 4 points for an ace, 3 points for a king, 2 points for a queen, and 1 point for a jack. These are usually referred to as "high card points." *These points have absolutely nothing to do with scoring.* They are purely a way to evaluate the strength of your hand.

Now that you know "how much money you can spend," you're ready to bid. It seems simple, right? It's not. Bridge has specific rules that govern what you can say and when you can say it. It's almost like learning another language. Learning to communicate this way will take up the bulk of the book.

Looking at the Suits

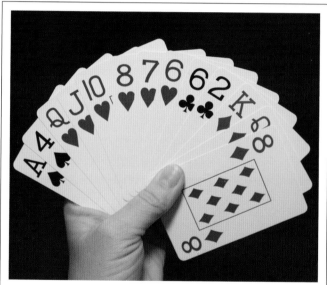

- Once you know your point count, you now want to identify your best suit. In this hand, hearts are your best suit.

- The reason you need to do this is that one suit will become the all-powerful

"trump" suit, and the more trump that you have, the more successful you will be.

- So, the bidding not only describes the value of your hand, but it also tells your partner what your best suit is.

The Four Ds

- Finally, someone will have "won" the auction.

- That person is called "the declarer." Now it's time to play the hand out.

- The partner of the declarer, the player opposite the

declarer, is called the "the dummy." After the lead, she puts all her cards on the table for everyone to see.

- The other two players are "the defenders."

PLAYING OUT THE HAND
All 52 cards get played one by one

Once the auction is over, the hand must be played out. The person to the left of the declarer puts out a card face up. This is called the lead. The lead may be any card at all. In other words, there are no rule-based restrictions, although there are certainly some strategies that you'll want to learn. Those I'll get into later.

The next player is the dummy. He puts all his cards on the table for all to see. The dummy is not allowed to play any card in this hand. All decisions about the dummy's hand must come from the declarer. If it's just a social game of bridge, some dummies will use the opportunity to leave the table for a few minutes.

So, now it's up to the declarer's dummy hand. He must "follow suit," which means playing a card in the same suit. Then

The Lead

- This player is on lead. The person to her right just won the auction, and spades have been declared the trump suit.

- This player isn't sure what to lead. Her partner didn't bid. She settles on the 4 of hearts.

- She pulls it out of her hand and places it face up on the table.

The Dummy

- After the lead, the dummy puts all her cards on the table for the other three players to see.

- The cards should be lined up in columns, in descending order, <u>except the trump suit should always be on</u> <u>the declarer's left</u>. The cards should be facing the declarer.

- Once the dummy puts her hand down, her job is done for that round.

the third player plays a card, and finally the declarer plays a card. Each player contributes 1 card in that suit. This is called a "trick." The player who owned the highest card in that suit is the winner of the trick. He collects the 4 cards and places them in front of him. He then leads to the next trick.

Play continues in this manner until all 13 tricks have been taken. The game is scored, and you move on to the next deal.

The First Trick

- The declarer gets to play both her hand and the dummy's hand, but she doesn't get to pick and choose where the cards come from. It must be a clockwise progression.

- Because hearts have been led, the declarer must now choose a heart from the dummy. She can choose the ace or the 2.

- She chooses the 2 from the dummy after looking at her hand. She knows she's going to have to play the king.

Continuing the Play

- Now this hand is halfway done.

- Notice that there are five tricks in front of the declarer and two tricks in front of one of the defenders.

- One defender collects all the tricks for the partnership so that they're kept together.

- They continue until all 13 cards have been played.

TRUMP

Trump is the all-powerful suit, and you want to be the one to choose it

Bridge is a game with a trump suit. The trump suit is a suit that is considered more powerful than the other suits. Many card games use this concept of trump. In the game of Spades, for instance, the spade suit is always the trump suit. In most games, however, the trump suit changes with each deal, either chosen randomly or chosen by a player.

In bridge, the trump suit is chosen by a player. During the bidding, the player not only describes the strength of his hand, but he also gives an indication of which suit he hopes will be the trump suit. The partnership tries to pick the suit that together gives them the most trump.

As I mentioned earlier, a player must follow suit throughout

Trumping In

- Assume that this is your hand. You are the fourth person to play a card in this trick.

- The 3 of hearts was led by your left hand opponent (LHO). Your partner played the queen, and your right hand opponent's (RHO) king covered it.

- You have no hearts to play. Clubs are trump. You have played the 2 of clubs to win the trick.

Discard Instead of Trumping

- This time your partner is winning the trick with the queen of hearts.

- You don't have any hearts, but you don't want to play a trump here, because your partnership has already won.

- In this case you want to throw off the 3 of spades.

- Even if you'd thrown the king of spades, your partner would still be winning with the queen of hearts.

the trick. If the first card of the trick is a heart, for example, everyone must play a heart. But what happens if you don't have a heart?

If you don't have the suit that is led, you may choose a card from any of the other three suits. If you choose a card from the trump suit, it will beat the rest of the cards in the trick, no matter what the number of the trump card (unless someone else is also out of that suit in which case the highest trump wins the trick). If clubs are trump, even the 2 of clubs will beat any other card in any other suit.

You aren't required to play trump. If your partner has played the highest card in the trick, and you don't have a card in that suit, you may throw off a card in another suit. In this case a card in another suit has no value whatsoever, no matter what its number. Unless it's a card from the trump suit, it cannot take the trick.

Overtrump

- Again, let's use your same hand.

- The 6 of hearts was led, and your partner covered with the queen of hearts. Your RHO has a different hand, with no hearts. So she trumped your partner's card with the 8 of clubs.

- In this case, you can't trump in with the 2 of clubs any more. You choose the 9 of clubs to win the trick.

Pulling Trump

- If you know you and your partner have a lot more trump than the opponents, then most of the time a good strategy would be to lead a trump.

- This is called "pulling trump," and it's usually done by the declarer.

- By taking the opponents' trump you reduce the possibility of them trumping in on the remaining tricks.

BIDDING RULES
Follow the strict bidding guidelines to get to the right bid

Now that you understand what a trick is and what the trump suit is, and you have a sense of how a hand is played out, let's talk about the rules for the bidding.

When you bid, you are only allowed to choose from a word bank of 15 words. The 15 words are pass, one, two, three, four, five, six, seven, clubs, diamonds, hearts, spades, double, redouble, and "no trump." (The phrase "no trump" could technically bring it to 16 words, but since you can't say one of them without the other, then we might as well keep it at 15.)

The auction begins with the dealer. The dealer analyzes his hand and decides whether or not he's interested in entering the auction based on the number of points in his hand. If he's not interested, he says "pass" and the bid moves clockwise to the next player. That person may either bid or pass.

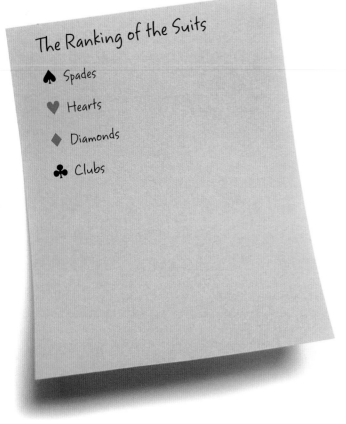

The Ranking of the Suits

♠ Spades

♥ Hearts

♦ Diamonds

♣ Clubs

The Book

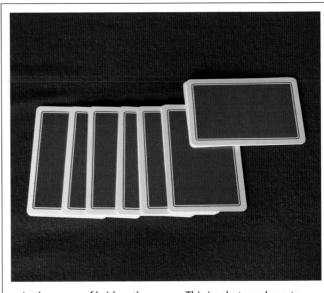

- In the game of bridge, they expect you to only enter the bidding if you think you can take more than half the tricks.

- These first 6 tricks are called "the book."

- This is what you have to take before you can start counting the tricks you got.

- So the "1" in the "1 heart" bid means "1 over book" or 7 tricks. You can't bid anything lower than 7 tricks.

Eventually someone will be interested in bidding. Let's say the third player has 13 high card points and a 6-card heart suit. He will say 1 heart. The "1" in this bid refers to the number of tricks he expects to take—more on that later—and the "heart" part of the bid indicates the suit that the bidder would prefer as the trump suit.

Now it's the next player's turn. He may pass or bid. If he wants to bid, he must bid higher than the previous bid. He can beat the previous bid by raising the number or bidding a higher suit, because the suits are ranked. Clubs are the lowest,

followed by diamonds, then hearts, then spades.

An easy way to remember the order of the suits is to realize that it's alphabetical, starting with the lowest ranked suit.

A 1 Heart Bid

- The player holding this hand would bid 1 ♥.

- Hearts is the best suit in this hand, and the bid starts at the lowest level—1—meaning 7 tricks.

- Here's the translation of 1 ♥ in English: "Partner, I'm comfortable saying that we can take 7 tricks if hearts are the trump suit."

The Next Bid

- The player with this hand is next clockwise around the table.

- If this player wants to bid, he will have to beat the 1 ♥ bid.

- He has two good suits. He could say 1 ♠, which beats the previous bid with a higher ranking suit. Or he could say 2 ♣, which beats the bid with more tricks.

- He may not say 1 ♣.

THE BIDDING CONTINUES

Players bid on, going higher and higher until there's a winner

If we build on the bidding we just described, the bids so far have been 1 ♥ and then 1 ♠. Bidding continues clockwise around the table, and it's now the partner of the 1 ♥ bidder who makes the next bid.

Because bridge is a partnership game, this person has more to think about than just what cards are in his hand. He has to think about what his partner has said as well. Remember that we translated the 1 ♥ bid into "I think we can make 7 tricks if hearts are trump." We can add a sentence to that now. It really means "I think we can make 7 tricks if hearts are trump, so how do you feel about hearts, partner?"

So the player looks at his hand. If his partner hadn't asked that question, he might have bid something different, but he first wants to take a look at his hearts. In other words, in polite

Using the Bidding Box

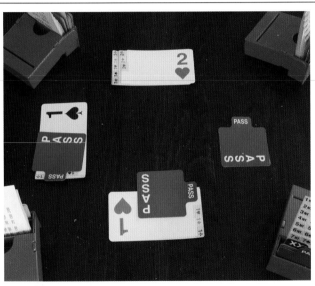

- Most casual bridge is bid verbally, with the players saying their bids out loud.

- At the higher levels of bridge, or in any duplicate bridge game, bidding boxes are used.

- This is what our bidding would look like if we had been using bidding boxes.

Bidding High Up

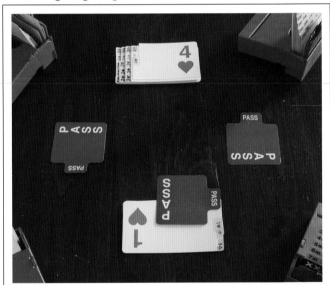

- In this auction, the opponents weren't bidding at all.

- The auction went 1 ♥ by the opener and then the partner went all the way to 4 ♥.

- This is where it differs from a regular auction where you want to get the cheapest bid possible.

- In bridge you are rewarded for bidding higher, even without competition.

conversation you really should answer a question before posing one of your own. He does like hearts, so he says 2 ♥, which beats the previous 1 ♠ bid.

The fourth and final player at the table now gets to bid. He has a terrible hand. He just says pass.

Bidding continues until there are three passes in a row. Once this happens, the last bid before the three passes is the winner of the auction. The suit he declared on that bid

is the trump suit, and he's required to get a certain number of tricks.

Three passes usually mean the auction is over, but if the first three bids are pass without the fourth player ever getting a chance to bid, he's allowed to bid. As soon as one player bids, however, then it's three passes and the auction is over.

The declarer

Competitive Bidding

- This auction had lots of bidding.

- The last bid before the three passes was 5 ♦. So diamonds are trump, and that partnership has committed to taking 11 of the 13 tricks (the book of 6 plus the 5 that was bid).

- The declarer is the player who "declared" the diamonds first, not the one who ended up with the last bid.

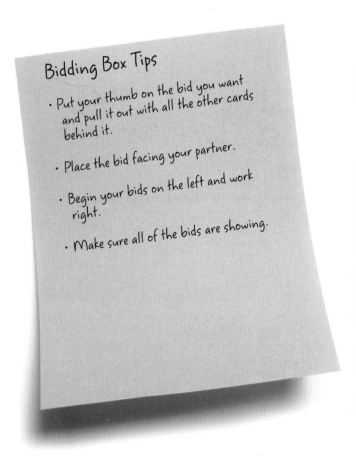

Bidding Box Tips

- Put your thumb on the bid you want and pull it out with all the other cards behind it.

- Place the bid facing your partner.

- Begin your bids on the left and work right.

- Make sure all of the bids are showing.

SCORING BASICS
All bridge scoring methods have a few things in common

There are actually several different ways to play bridge, depending on how many players you have and what type of scoring you use. The bidding and the playing rules are all the same, but it's really the scoring that makes all the difference.

In its earliest days, bridge had one way of scoring. That type is known as contract bridge, auction bridge, or most commonly, rubber bridge.

At the same time as the game was exploding in popularity, it was also gathering a following of players who wanted to remove the influence of the "luck of the cards." Because the game is such an intellectual challenge, it was very frustrating to lose—not because of poor playing or bidding, but merely because you weren't dealt good cards that day. Duplicate bridge—and a new way to score—was born.

Scoring Your Tricks

- Now you have to score. Refer back to the auction. How many tricks did you say you'd take?

- Let's say you bid 2 ♠— meaning the 6 tricks for book, plus 2 more—in other words, 8 tricks.

- If you won 8 tricks, you get the score. If you only got 7, the defenders get the score.

- Only one pair gets the score on each hand.

The Majors

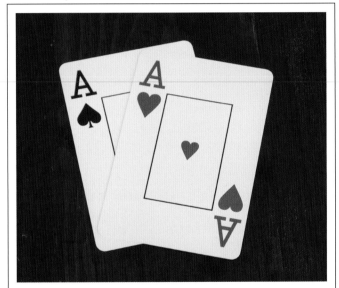

- As you know, the suits are ranked. Spades and hearts are the two higher ranked suits. These are called the majors.

- If you choose a major for trump, you get 30 points per trick.

- The tricks in the "book" do not count toward scoring.

- So if you bid 2 ♠ and make 2 ♠, you get 60 points. 2x30 = 60.

Duplicate required at least two tables, though, so players who liked that scoring but only had one table used something called Chicago scoring.

And finally, for those players who are interested in a purely social game but end up with more than four players, a version called social bridge evolved.

Despite all these different ways of scoring the game, there are some things about the scoring that all types have in common: Only one pair at a time can score, the majors are worth 30 points a trick, the minors are worth 20 points a trick, and no trump is 40 for the first trick and 30 for every subsequent trick.

Duplicate scoring was further honed to include scoring and games with names such as IMPS, Victory Points, Board-a-Match, Knockouts, and Swiss Teams.

The Minors

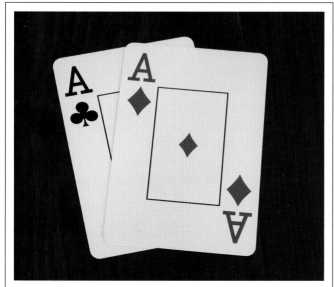

- Clubs and diamonds are referred to as the minors.

- If you choose a minor to be trump, you get 20 points per trick.

- If you bid 2 ♦ and make 2 ♦, you get 40 points. 2x20 = 40.

- If you bid 2 ♦, but make 4 over book (10 tricks), then you also get to count the 40 points for the 2 overtricks.

No Trump

- Sometimes a pair is going to choose to play without a trump suit (more on that later).

- If a pair plays in no trump (NT) then it's 40 points for the first trick over book and 30 points for every subsequent trick.

- If you bid 3NT and make 3NT then it's 40+30+30 = 100.

13

GETTING TO GAME

After you score points for each trick, what happens?

Understanding the scoring is vital to understanding the bidding. Take some time to really grasp the scoring part of the game, because otherwise you may not comprehend why some bids are better than others.

So here's a little summary of your scoring knowledge so far:

1. You know you get 20, 30, or 40 points for a trick, depending on what you bid.

2. You know that the tricks taken for the book do not count toward the score.

3. You also know that if you underbid, you still get the points for the tricks that you take that are over what you bid.

4. And finally, you know that if you don't make your bid, the defenders will get the points.

So now you're probably assuming that players only bid

Scoring Affects Bidding

- In this hand, you have five clubs and five spades.

- Because you know that minors are only worth 20 points, and majors are worth 30 points, you know it's better to bid the spades even though the jack is your highest spade.

- You'll still win some tricks with the high clubs, but this way you'll get 30 points per trick, not just 20 points per trick.

Bidding to Game

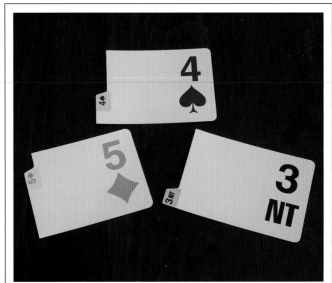

- Bidding 4 of a major gets you to game, because 4x30 = 120, which is over 100. You have to take 10 of the 13 tricks.

- Bidding 5 of a minor gets you to game, because 5x20 = 100, which is the goal. You have to take 11 tricks.

- Bidding 3 of no trump is game, because 40+30+30 = 100. You have to take 9 tricks.

as high as they need to in order to win the bid, just as you would in a regular auction. This would be a good assumption if the game of bridge didn't throw in another wrinkle—getting to game.

In bridge, you get rewarded if you reach 100 points as a declarer. The actual reward differs depending on which type of bridge you're playing, but in each type, the reward is significant and the goal of 100 points is the same. This is referred to as "bidding game" or "getting to game."

So if you bid 2 ♥, you get 60 points (2x30). However, if you

bid 4 ♥, you get 120, which is over 100 and therefore you reached game. Now you get the big reward.

So the question you probably have now is what if you bid 2 ♥ and make 4 ♥? In that case, you get 2x30 = 60 (your bid). It's not over 100. You don't get your reward. However, you still get to keep the extra 60 points for the two extra tricks. If you don't bid game than you don't get the reward even if you make game.

Getting Set

- If you don't reach your contract, it's called "getting set."

- In this case, the defenders get the points. Only one pair gets points on a hand.

- The defenders don't get points for their tricks. They get points for the tricks

- you *didn't* get but said you would in the auction.

- If you bid 4 ♥ (10 tricks), and make only 3 (9 tricks), the defenders get points for 1 trick. You don't get any credit for the 9 tricks you did get.

Defender Scoring

- The defenders get 50 points—no matter which suit is trump—for each trick that the declarer is short in their contract.

- If the declarer bid 4 ♥, but made only 3, he is short 1 trick. The defenders get 50

- points. If he was short by 3, the defenders get 150 points.

- Defenders cannot "get to game" so getting over 100 points doesn't give them anything extra.

RUBBER BRIDGE
Bridge the way it was originally intended

Rubber bridge is the original way that bridge was scored. At its most basic level, the score sheet features two columns, with a line across the middle. More complicated rubber bridge score sheets could include several columns at once, places for the names of the players, or scoring cheat sheets.

In rubber bridge, the object of the game is to have amassed more points than your opponents at the end of the rubber.

The rubber is over after one side makes two games.

Players deal, bid, and play the game as previously described. Let's say a player has bid and made three hearts. She gets 90 points. These points go *below* the line in the middle of the paper. If she and her partner get 30 points on the next hand, they now have 120 points below the line. This is over 100, so they have won their first game.

Partial Game with Overtrick

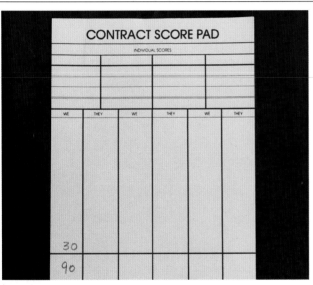

- In the first deal, the Team 1 partnership bid 3 ♥, but made 4.

- They multiply their bid (3) times the value of a major (30 points a trick), to come up with 90 points. This goes below the line.

- However, once they played, they were able to make one more trick than they bid. This goes above the line.

- The defenders get nothing.

Defender Scoring

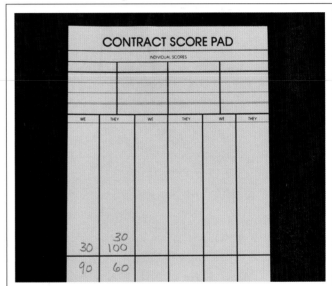

- In the second deal, Team 1 bids 3 ♥ again, but this time ♥ are set by 2 tricks. Here, the defense (Team 2) gets the points. They get 50 points per trick (50+50 = 100), which goes above the line.

- In the third hand, Team 2 wins a 2 ♠ bid. They make 3 ♠, so they get 60 below the line (2x30) for their bid and 30 above the line for the overtrick.

- Now both teams have a score underneath the line that is less than 100, so neither team has won game.

If they get any over tricks, they go *above* the line. Any points earned for setting the opponents go above the line as well. The above-the-line points still count toward the point total, but they don't count toward getting a game.

Once a team gets two games, they get a bonus for winning the rubber. If they've won two games in a row, they get a 700-point bonus. If the other team also has a game, then the

Team 2 still gets to keep their 60 points, but it no longer counts toward a new game. Everyone starts over at zero underneath this new line.

winners of the rubber only get a 500-point bonus. This goes above the line.

Now the players add up all the points in their column. The team with the most points has won that rubber. Most rubber bridge players play more than one rubber. The most common choice is to play three rubbers so that each player can have a rubber with each of the other three players. Players keep their individual score, and at the end of the three rubbers, it's the player who has the highest cumulative score who is the sole winner.

Making Game

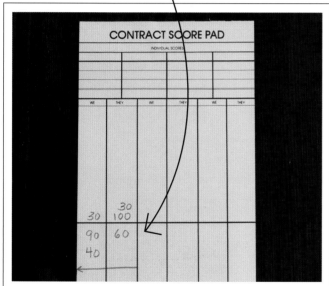

- In the fourth deal, Team 1 bids 2 ♣ and makes exactly 2 ♣.

- They multiply their bid (2) times the value of a minor (20 points a trick), to come up with 40 points. Again, this goes below the line.

- Now this partnership has 90 points and 40 points below the line, which has allowed them to reach their goal of 100 points below the line.

- Draw a line across the two columns. This is the new line under which the scores are placed. Team 1 has won the made game.

Both Sides Have a Game

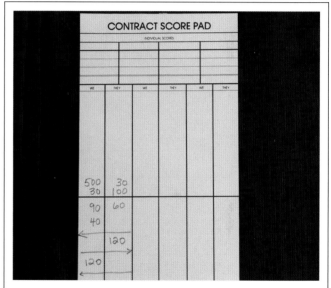

- Team 2 bids 4 ♠ and makes it. This counts for 120 points, which means they've reached a game on only one deal.

- Both teams now have a game. This means they are both "vulnerable," which means that the defense gets 100 points per trick if

they are set. This happens in the sixth deal, which is set 2 tricks.

- Next, Team 1 bids and makes 4 ♥, getting their second game.

- They have won that rubber and get a bonus score of 500 points.

17

DUPLICATE SCORING
Taking the luck of the cards out of the game

Many rubber bridge players loved the game but were frustrated by the fact that getting dealt a string of bad cards could cause a top pair to lose to a weak pair no matter how brilliant their playing was.

Enter duplicate bridge. While rubber bridge can be played with only four players, duplicate bridge must have at least eight players—four at each table. Both tables play the exact same hands and you win points based on how you did compared to the other table. In other words, you are really competing against the pair at the other table sitting in the same direction as you are.

The cards are kept in duplicate trays. After a table plays the hand, the tray is passed to another table to play the hand. A compass is on the tray indicating north, south, east, and west

Duplicate-Style Play

- In order for everyone to play the same hand, the cards need to be kept separate.

- After a trick, each player places his card facedown in front. The ends of the card point toward the pair that won that trick.

- At the end of the hand, the player picks up his 13 cards and puts them back into his slot on the board.

- The game is scored and the board and score pad are passed to another table.

Duplicate Scoring Sheet

ACBL SHORT TRAVELING SCORE
(Mitchell or Howell)

North player keeps score.
Enter E-W Pair No.

Board No. 7

N-S Pair No.	Contract	BY	Made	Down	SCORE N-S	SCORE E-W	N-S Match Points	E-W Pair No.	E-W Match Points
1	4S	N	4		420			3	
2	3S	N	3		140			5	
3									
4									
5									
6									
7									
8									
9									
10									

- This is typical of a scoring sheet used in a duplicate game.

- Pair 1 bid 4 ♠ and made 4 ♠. 4x20 = 120. This is over 100 (game) so they get a game bonus of 300 (not vulnerable).

- The Pair 2 players only bid 3 ♠ and made only 3 ♠, *with the same exact cards.*

- They get 90 points (3x30 = 90) plus a 50-point bonus for making their bid for a total of 140 points.

so that the direction of the cards stays the same.

In duplicate bridge, each hand is scored in isolation. If you don't bid game, you can't save the 60 points you earned from the first deal and apply it toward the next deal's effort to get to game. Also, since no one would ever become "vulnerable," the trays are marked artificially: In a group of four trays, one will have no one vulnerable, one will have both pairs vulnerable, and the other two will alternate which pair is vulnerable.

Because each hand is scored by itself, the scoring by necessity must be a little different. If you don't bid game but you make your contract, you get your partial score plus 50 points for making the contract. If you do bid game, you get your trick score, plus a 300-point bonus if you are not vulnerable and a 500-point bonus if you are vulnerable.

Not Bidding Game

ACBL SHORT TRAVELING SCORE
(Mitchell or Howell)

North player keeps score.
Enter E-W Pair No.

Board No. 7

N-S Pair No.	Contract	BY	Made	Down	SCORE N-S	SCORE E-W	N-S Match Points	E-W Pair No.	E-W Match Points
1	4 S	N	4		420			3	
2	3 S	N	3		140			5	
3	3 S	N	4		170			2	
4									
5									
6									
7									
8									
9									

- Pair 3 made 4 ♠ like Pair 1. They, however, didn't bid the game. They only bid 3 ♠.

- They got 90 points (3x30) plus 50 for making their bid, plus 30 points for the extra trick. 90+50+30 = 170.

- Pair 1 and Pair 3 played the game equally well, but Pair 1 were rewarded for better bidding.

More Tricks, Lower Score

ACBL SHORT TRAVELING SCORE
(Mitchell or Howell)

North player keeps score.
Enter E-W Pair No.

Board No. 7

N-S Pair No.	Contract	BY	Made	Down	SCORE N-S	SCORE E-W	N-S Match Points	E-W Pair No.	E-W Match Points
1	4 S	N	4		420			3	
2	3 S	N	3		140			5	
3	3 S	N	4		170			2	
4	3 S	N	5		200			4	
5									
6									
7									
8									
9									
10									

- At the fourth table, Pair 4 also bid 3 ♠ like the previous two tables. They, however, made 5 ♠.

- Their scoring was 90 (3x30) plus 50 (making their bid bonus) plus 60 (two overtricks, which is 2x30), which equals 200.

- Pair 4 played the hand better than anyone, but they still didn't beat Pair 1, who bid game and made game.

MORE DUPLICATE INTRICACIES
More to think about when you're playing duplicate bridge

Using our same five tables, let's say the fifth North/South pair for our example board bid 4 ♠ but only made 3 (in other words, 9 tricks). In that case, the East/West pair they were playing against would get the score. They would get 50 points, because the North/South pair was short one trick. The North/South pair would then have nothing written in their column, but if it helps you to grasp the concept, it's as if they

had a -50 written in their column. At the end of the duplicate bridge session—usually about three hours—the slip of paper is taken out of the board, and the scores are then given "match play" points. They get 1 point for every pair they beat. Pairs get a half a point if they tie another pair.

So, for our example, the pair with the highest score beat four tables and get 4 points. The pair with the next highest

Getting Set

ACBL SHORT TRAVELING SCORE
(Mitchell or Howell)
North player keeps score.
Enter E-W Pair No.

Board No. 7

N-S Pair No.	Contract	BY	Made	Down	SCORE N-S	SCORE E-W	N-S Match Points	E-W Pair No.	E-W Match Points
1	4 S	N	4		420			3	
2	3 S	N	3		140			5	
3	3 S	N	4		170			2	
4	3 S	N	5		200			4	
5	4 S	N		1		50		1	
6									
7									
8									
9									
10									

- The fifth table bid 4 ♠, like Pair 1, but they only made 3 ♠.

- Their bidding was just as good, but their play was not. Or maybe their opponents' defense was better. Who knows?

- In this case, the East/West pair gets the score. They get 50 points.

- Picture it as -50 for the North/South pair.

Matchpoint Scoring

ACBL SHORT TRAVELING SCORE
(Mitchell or Howell)
North player keeps score.
Enter E-W Pair No.

Board No. 7

N-S Pair No.	Contract	BY	Made	Down	SCORE N-S	SCORE E-W	N-S Match Points	E-W Pair No.	E-W Match Points
1	4 S	N	4		420		4	3	
2	3 S	N	3		140		1	5	
3	3 S	N	4		170		2	2	
4	3 S	N	5		200		3	4	
5	4 S	N		1		50	0	1	
6									
7									
8									
9									
10									

- Now the individual scores are compared with the scores at the other tables and given "match points."

- As you can see, Pair 1 gets 4 points, Pair 2 gets 1 point, Pair 3 gets 2 points, Pair 4 gets 3 points, and Pair 5 gets 0 points.

- As much as Pair 1 would like to take their 420 points, it's only their 4 points that actually goes on the score pad in the end.

score get 3 points, and so on. The pair that didn't beat anyone get 0 points for that board.

Once each board is scored for match play points, then the match points are all added together. Pair 1 got 4 points on that board. Let's say they played ten boards, and these were their scores: 4, 1.5, 2, 2, 2, 2.5, 1, 3, 4, 0. Pair 1's score for that session would be 22. Comparing these final scores gives you the winner for the day. In big game, there's a North/South winner, an East/West winner, and an overall winner.

Scoring for East/West

ACBL SHORT TRAVELING SCORE
(Mitchell or Howell)

North player keeps score.
Enter E-W Pair No.

Board No. 7

N-S Pair No.	Contract	BY	Made	Down	SCORE N-S	SCORE E-W	N-S Match Points	E-W Pair No.	E-W Match Points
1	4 S	N	4		420		4	3	
2	3 S	N	3		140		1	5	
3	3 S	N	4		170		2	2	
4	3 S	N	5		200		3	4	
5	4 S	N		1		50	0	1	
6									
7									
8									
9									
10									
11									

- Up to now, we've been scoring for the North/South pairs. The East/West pairs also get a score for each board.

- The second to last column on the score pad has a place for the East/West pair

to put their pair numbers. This is important, since East/West is changing tables every few hands.

- The last column is for the match points for the East/West teams.

Matchpoints for East/West

ACBL SHORT TRAVELING SCORE
(Mitchell or Howell)

North player keeps score.
Enter E-W Pair No.

Board No. 7

N-S Pair No.	Contract	BY	Made	Down	SCORE N-S	SCORE E-W	N-S Match Points	E-W Pair No.	E-W Match Points
1	4 S	N	4		420		4	3	0
2	3 S	N	3		140		1	5	3
3	3 S	N	4		170		2	2	2
4	3 S	N	5		200		3	4	1
5	4 S	N		1		50	0	1	4
6									
7									
8									
9									
10									

- The highest scoring East/West team is Pair 4, who was the only pair to get a positive score in the East/West column. They get 4 points.

- Even though they didn't have the cards to win the

bid, they were able to defend the best with the cards they were dealt.

- The next highest was Pair 3. As defenders, they gave the fewest points to their opponents—140 points. And so on.

SCORING EXTRAS
Chicago bridge, party bridge, and a few other scoring details

Contract bridge is largely divided into two groups: the rubber bridge purists and the duplicate fanatics. Each will staunchly defend its own favorite way of playing the game. Nonetheless, there are still two more ways to score—Chicago bridge and party bridge—though both are primarily based on duplicate scoring.

Chicago bridge is for duplicate fans who find themselves

with only four players. Party bridge is a social way to play bridge with eight or twelve players. You change partners, opponents, and tables every couple of hands.

The scoring is already so complicated that I'm sure you can't imagine that there's any more, but before we leave the scoring chapter and move on to bidding, playing, and defending strategies, there are probably a few other key scoring aspects

Chicago Scoring

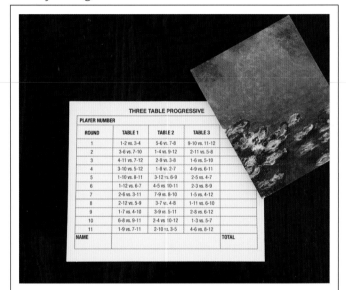

- Four hands are played with the same partner. In the first hand no one is vulnerable, in the next two hands the dealer is vulnerable, and in the last hand all are.

- Scoring is the same as duplicate, without the match point part.

- After four hands, players switch partners. Players keep their individual score. After twelve hands, the player with the highest score wins.

Party Bridge

- Everyone gets a number. The tally lists who plays with whom.

- For instance, in this example, at Table 1, Player 1 plays with Player 6 against Players 2 and 5, while 3 and 8 play against 4 and 7 at Table 2.

- After two hands, players move according to the numbers on the tally.

- Players keep their own scores and total them up at the end of the night.

of contract bridge that need to be addressed. (Please refer to the handy scoring summary in the Resource Directory for a more succinct scoring reference.)

As I'm sure you can imagine, it's very difficult to take 12 or 13 tricks in a hand. Because that's such a challenge, the game rewards those players who are bold enough to go for it. Bidding and winning 13 tricks is called a "grand slam" and bidding and winning 12 tricks is referred to as a "small slam." You get extra bonus points for this.

The final scoring detail involves the "double" and "redouble"

bids. A pair may choose to double another pair when they don't believe the other pair can make what they bid. Similarly, a pair who has just been doubled in the bidding process, may redouble if they believe they can make their bid. If a contract is doubled, then the scoring team gets double the points. If it's redoubled, it's quadruple the points.

Bidding Slam

- Some hands are so strong that you try to get some extra bonus points by bidding slam.

- If you bid and make a grand slam, you get 1,000 extra points if you're not vulnerable and 1,500 points if you are.

- If you bid and make a small slam, you get 500 extra points if you're not vulnerable and 750 points if you are.

Double and Redouble

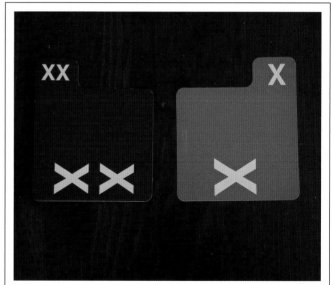

- Occasionally the opponents bid up too high or get in the wrong trump suit.

- If you feel that this is the case, you say double (symbolized by the X) when it's your turn to bid.

- If you set them, you get double the points. If they make it, though, they get extra points.

- The opponents can also bid redouble (symbolized by the XX), which just doubles the double—for even higher point counts.

EVALUATING YOUR HAND
Count up your points and decide whether or not you should bid

You already know how to evaluate the strength of your hand: 4 points for an ace, 3 points for a king, 2 points for a queen, and 1 point for a jack. Now you're actually going to put that information to good use.

If you consider that each suit has those 4 cards, and you add up those 4 cards (4+3+2+1 = 10), you realize that each suit has a possible 10 points. Since there are four suits, there are

40 total points in a deck. Take it a step further. If there are four of you sitting around a table, then you can divide those 40 points by the four people and realize that an average hand has about 10 points.

Remember that the rules of bridge require you to take half the tricks—your book—before you can count the tricks you bid. So if you and your partner need to take more than half

Bidding a Hand

- This hand has 14 points. You can bid this hand.

- Now look at your best suit. Is it spades or clubs? The spades have more high cards, but the clubs are longer.

- Remember, you want to have at least 5 cards in a suit if you're going to bid it.

- So for this hand you would say 1 ♣.

Two Matching Suits

- This hand has 15 points. You definitely want to bid this hand.

- In this hand the spades and clubs both have 5 cards. How do you choose which suit to bid?

- Remember that major suits are worth 30 points and minor suits are worth only 20.

- So your best bid is 1 ♠.

the tricks, you can figure that you'll probably want to have more than half the points between you. Because of this, most beginning bridge players are advised to have at least 13 points—a better than average hand—in order to open the bidding. And you also want to have a long suit, because that's what you're choosing to be trump.

If you have 13 points and a 5-card or longer suit, you may open the bidding. Let's say your suit is hearts. You want to bid 1 ♥.

YELLOW ● **LIGHT**

More experienced players will use 12 points for an opening hand, but I don't advise it for beginners. Not only is 1 extra point helpful, but 13 is easier to remember. The number 13 already plays a big role in bridge. There are 13 cards in each suit, and there are 13 total tricks in each hand.

BASIC BIDDING

Many Points

- This hand has 18 points. It's a very strong hand. Almost half of the points in the whole deck are in this one hand. What do you bid?

- You still want to bid 1 of your best suit.

- In this case, you would bid 1 ♥.

Not Enough Points

- This hand has a beautiful heart suit, but you only have 9 points.

- The rest of the hand is pretty terrible.

- Your bid here is no bid. In other words, you want to say pass. You would be able to help your partner if she bids hearts.

RESPONDING
Your partner has bid, so now what do you do?

The bidding starts with the dealer, who can either bid or pass. Let's say the dealer—your partner—bids 1 ♥. In the world of bridge, we say he has "opened" the bidding. The next player (clockwise) passes. Now it's your turn.

Because your partner bid, you automatically become the "responder." The term *responder* is an especially apt term, because your bid will really be responding—in bridge language—to the question your partner just posed. The 1 ♥ bid translates to "Partner, I have at least 13 points and at least 5 hearts. Do you think hearts are a good trump suit for us and do you think we should go any higher?"

So the first dilemma you have is to decide whether the suit is a good one for trump. Obviously you're going to want to have more trump than the opponents, but how much more?

The Golden Fit

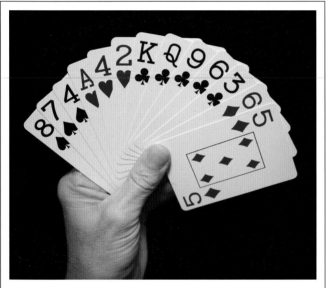

- Eight cards between you and your partner is often referred to as the "golden fit."

- If your partner has bid 1 ♠ and this is your hand, you will be happy to have spades be trump.

- He has five spades, you have three—the golden fit!

- Don't bother to mention your clubs. Spades are a major. Clubs are a minor.

Choices

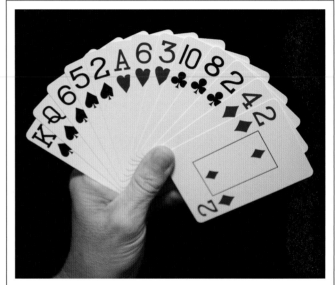

- This time your partner has bid 1 ♣.

- You have three clubs, but you also have a beautiful spade suit.

- You both would rather be in a major than a minor, so this time you would mention your spades first before supporting your partner.

- Because spades are a higher ranked suit, you say 1 ♠.

If you have 7 cards in that suit and your opponents have 6, is that enough? Most bridge players would say no, preferring at least 8, which would leave the opponents with only 5. Eight to 5 is a considerably bigger advantage than 7 to 6.

So, if you have at least 3 cards in your partner's suit, the next step would be to tell him the strength of your hand. Should you stay in 1 ♥ or bid 2 ♥, 3 ♥, or 4 ♥ so you can get a game? Can you make a grand slam?

If you don't have a fit, then you need to try a different suit. Do you have a 5-card suit? Maybe your partner will have 3 in that.

Searching for a Fit

- Your partner has bid 1 ♥. But this time you don't have the support.

- You do, however, have a spade suit. You bid 1 ♠.

- Now your partner bids 2 ♣. This means he doesn't like your spades. Do you like his second suit?

- Yes, you two should be in clubs.

No Trump

- Sometimes you and your partner struggle to find a suit that works for both of you.

- If you can't find the fit, it's probably better not to have any suit be trump.

- In bridge, you can actually bid no trump (NT), and it means just that: no trumping. High card wins in the suit that was led.

WEAK RESPONSES
What to bid when you don't have very many points

The rule of thumb is that you should have at least 6 points to respond. If your partner has 13 and you have 6 points, you have at least 19 points between the two of you, which means the opponents have at most 21. And remember, even if the opponents do have 2 more points than you, you're the ones picking the trump suit, so your chance of taking more tricks goes up a bit.

So 6 is generally accepted as the minimum number of points you need to respond to your partner, and the range for a weak, but biddable hand is 6 to 9 points. If you have fewer than 6 points, you just say pass.

Your partner has bid 1 ♥, and you have a weak hand. Your response would be 2 ♥. Translation: "Yes, partner, hearts would be a good trump suit, but I have a weak hand—at

Bust Hand

- This is a terrible hand.

- Yes, you have the hearts needed to support your partner, but you only have 2 points.

- You should pass.

- It's unlikely that you'll be able to even add 1 trick, so you don't want to be up any higher than your partnership has already committed.

Bust Hand No Fit

- This, too, is a terrible hand, but this time you don't even have heart support.

- Resist the temptation to bid the spades, even though passing would feel like you're hanging your partner out to dry.

- If you have a bust hand, chances are that the opponents are going to be bidding.

least 6 points but no more than 9 points."

When the bidding gets back to your partner, she'll take the information, combine it with what she knows about her hand, and decide if you should just stay where you are or maybe think about trying to bid game.

But let's say you don't have a fit. With a weak hand (6 to 9 points), you can feel comfortable changing suits, as long as you stay on the one level. In the 1 ♥ example, you could say 1 ♠ or you could say 1NT (no trump is ranked the highest).

You could not go to clubs or diamonds because you would have to bid it on the two level. This raises the number of tricks you have to earn, and you still may not have a fit. Your partner will keep bidding and you may get up too high.

Weak Hand (6 to 9 Points)

- Your partner has bid 1 ♥.

- This is your hand, and it has only 7 points. It's a weak hand, but since it does have three hearts, and you have between 6 and 9 points, you should raise your partner's bid to 2 ♥.

- You can feel confident that your hand can add at least one more trick.

Weak Hand No Fit

- Your partner has bid 1 ♥.

- You have a weak hand—only 7 points—but this time you can't support your partner's hearts.

- If you had a spade suit, you would bid 1 ♠, but you don't have that either. In fact, not only do you not have points, but you don't have a long suit.

- In this case, 1NT is the perfect bid.

AVERAGE HANDS
What to respond when you have a 10-, 11-, or 12-point hand

When you have a few more points, you have a lot more flexibility. Now when your partner bids, you can feel comfortable changing suits on the two level. It gives you more opportunities to find the suit that's right for you both. More points also means you have more of a chance to get to game once you do find a fit. And it also means that the opponents don't have as many points and probably won't be interfering with your

bidding. It's all good.

So let's start by assuming you have a fit right off the bat. Your partner bids 1 ♥, and you have three hearts in your hand and 11 points. It's not enough to say 2 ♥. Your partner will know you have the heart fit, but she'll think you are a weak hand with only 6 to 9 points. You want to be more encouraging than that. So your bid here is 3 ♥.

Average Hand (10 to 12 Points)

- Your partner has bid 1 ♥.

- This hand has 11 points. You want to bid 3 ♥, telling your partner that you have an average hand.

- If your partner has a few extra points over the 13 points he needed to open the bidding, he'll probably bid 4 ♥, which is game.

- If he doesn't have anything extra, he'll just pass.

Average Hand No Fit

- After your partner's opening bid of 1 ♥, you would bid 1 ♠ with this hand.

- The 1 ♠ bid doesn't show your points yet because you could have made the same bid with only 6 points.

- But your partner will bid again.

- When the responder changes suit, the opener MUST bid again for this very reason.

You may wonder why you would want to bid higher than you have to. Remember that you want to score as many points as possible, so if you have a chance at bidding game, you want to go for it. By telling your partner you have between 10 and 12 points, you may help her make the decision to go to game. More on that later. Now move on to a hand where you don't have a fit. Your partner bids 1 ♥. You can bid 1 ♠, 2 ♣, or 2 ♦—much more flexibility. Notice I didn't offer 1NT. When it's a response, the 1NT is a very weak bid, showing 6 to 9 points and the inability to go to the two level.

Going to the Two Level

- Your partner has bid 1 ♥.

- Since you have 11 points, you can feel comfortable going up another level to show your diamond suit. Bid 2 ♦.

- Your partner now knows that you have 10 or more points, because you took it up a level.

- And because you changed suits, he will bid again.

No Suit to Bid

It is likely that a balanced hand like this will end up in no trump.

- Your partner bid 1 ♥.

- You can't support the hearts, but you also don't have a suit to bid. You don't want to bid 1NT, because that shows a weak hand.

- With a hand like this, you should bid 2 ♣, indicat-

ing that your partner must choose a suit or bid no trump.

- Ideally you'd like to have a 5-card suit, but the opener should always anticipate that the responder might only have 4 in a suit.

BIG HANDS
What to do when you have 13 or more points in your hand

As I mentioned earlier, 13 points is a magic number in bridge. It's the number you need to open your hand and double the number you need to get to game in a major. To put it more plainly, if you and your partner have 26 points between the two of you, then you can bid to the four level. In hearts and spades, the four level is game.

So if your partner opens the bidding, and you're the responder sitting across from him with at least 13 points, you know that you should be in game: 13+13 = 26. For game in no trump, you should also have 26 points, even though you're only bidding to the three level. You need the extra points because you don't have the power of a trump suit. To bid game in a minor, which is at the five level (11 of the 13 tricks), you really should have 29 points. That's a lot of points

Opening Hand (13+ Points)

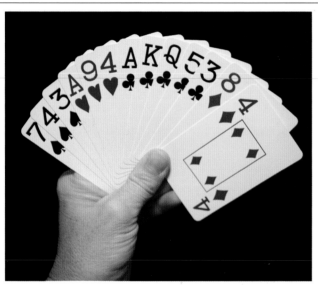

- Your partner has said 1 ♥.

- If he hadn't opened the bidding, you would have opened when your turn came around.

- You know now that you have enough points to be in game.

- Because you have so many points, you have room to play around a bit. Tell your partner about your club suit before you jump to four ♥.

Opening Hand No Fit

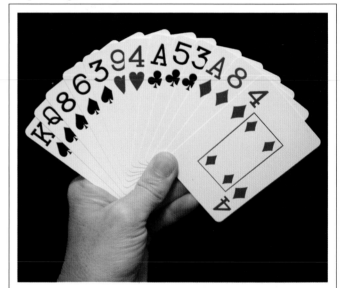

- Your partner said 1 ♥.

- Your response here is 1 ♠, even though you could have made the same bid with only 6 points.

- There's no need to rush to show your strong hand.

- Changing suits on the one level shows 6 or more points. You haven't limited your hand on the other end.

and a lot of tricks, which is why most players work hard to find that major or no trump bid.

To bid a small slam, you want roughly 33 points. To bid a grand slam, you want 37 points. When you have a big hand and your partner opens first, all these possibilities should flash into your head—think about how far you can go successfully.

········· GREEN ● LIGHT ··············

To practice evaluating your hand, bidding, and responding, sit down with a deck of cards and deal yourself some hands. Seeing the different combinations in front of you will help you to grasp the bidding better.

Slam Hand

- This hand is so strong that once you hear your partner make an opening bid, you know that you're going to be bidding slam.

- Remember that your partner doesn't know how big your hand is, so you can't make a passable bid. You must change suits.

- Later in this book you'll learn more strategies for getting to slam. Point counts help, but they aren't everything.

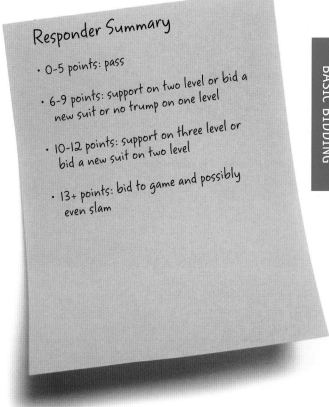

Responder Summary

- 0-5 points: pass

- 6-9 points: support on two level or bid a new suit or no trump on one level

- 10-12 points: support on three level or bid a new suit on two level

- 13+ points: bid to game and possibly even slam

BASIC BIDDING

BACK TO THE OPENER
What to do after the responder answers your question

Until there are three passes in a row, the bidding continues, so if you're the opening bidder, you should anticipate bidding more than once.

If your partner supports your suit, it's easy. You add your points plus her points to see if you can get to game. If you can, you jump to game. If you can't, you pass. This is why it's important for the responder to be specific with her point count.

As opener, you can also invite your partner to game. Let's say you bid 1 ♥ and your partner bids 2 ♥. She has 6 to 9 points, plus heart support. You have 17 points. If she has the top of her bid—9 points—then you have game, but if she has the bottom, then you're probably a little short of game. This is where you invite her to game. You say 3 ♥. In the bridge language this translates to, "I know you have 6 to 9 points.

1 ♥, 2 ♥

- You opened with 1 ♥ with this hand, and your partner responded with 2 ♥.

- You know she has between 6 and 9 points. You add the most she could have (9 points) to your 13 and you

- only get to 22 points. This is not enough for game, so you just pass.

- She didn't change suits, so you're not forced to bid again.

Second Suit

- In this hand, you bid 1 ♥ and your partner responded 1 ♠.

- She doesn't like your hearts and you don't like her spades. Your bid now is 2 ♦.

- Your partner should expect no more than 4 cards in your second suit.

If you only have 6 or 7, pass. If you have 8 or 9, I have some extra points, and I think we can be in game."

It's harder if you don't have a fit. If your partner bids another suit, try to support her. If you can't and you have at least 4 cards in another suit, bid that or go to no trump if your hand is balanced. Avoid bidding your hearts again unless you have more than five. A rebid of the same suit tells your partner that the suit is longer than he originally assumed. You are saying, "Actually I have six hearts, partner. Maybe we can get to the golden fit with 6+2. Do you have two hearts?"

Going to No Trump

- With the hand changed slightly, you have no second suit to bid.

- You can't rebid your hearts. You know your partner doesn't like them.

- You bid 1NT.

Rebidding Your Suit

- You bid 1 ♥ and your partner responded 1 ♠.

- Since you have three spades, you can probably support your partner, but he might only have a 4-card suit.

- Do you have a better option? You do. You have an extra heart that your partner doesn't know about.

- Your bid is 2 ♥.

35

NO SUIT TO BID
When you have opening points, but you don't have a 5-card suit

In the old days of bridge, you just went ahead and bid your longest suit, regardless of how many cards were in it (given that there are 13 cards in your hand, you would always have at least one 4-card suit). But as bridge bidding became more refined, players who could be more specific about the number of cards in a suit tended to be more successful.

Also, as duplicate bridge became more popular, it became

critical to find a trump fit in the majors rather than the minors. Both of these developments changed standard bidding practices rather dramatically. It also made learning to bid a whole lot more complicated.

So right now, you know you have to have 5 cards to bid a suit. We're going to refine that a little: You have to have 5 cards to bid a major suit—hearts or spades. Because not all

Convenient Minor

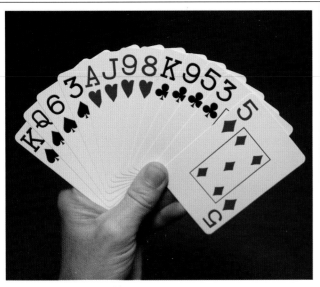

- In this hand, you can't bid your hearts or your spades because you don't have five of them.

- You don't have five clubs either, but we don't care about the minor suits any more.

- Your bid is 1 ♣. This bid is asking your partner for a 4-card major. It is not about your clubs.

Choosing the Minor Suit

- If one suit is longer, that's the one you choose— choose length over strength.

- But it may be the case that you don't have a better minor.

- In a situation where you have two 3 card suits, you choose clubs.

- This bid is 1 ♣.

hands will have a 5-card major, you're going to have to learn your first convention—the convenient minor convention.

A convention is an artificial bid used to convey information. For this convention, we use the minor suits to help us find a fit in the major suits. Imagine you have four spades. You can't bid 1 ♠ because you'd be promising five spades. But maybe your partner also has four spades, and you could have the golden fit if only you were allowed to bid them. This is where the convenient minor comes in.

From here on out, when you say 1 ♣ or 1 ♦, you are not saying you have five of that suit. You are saying, "Partner, I don't have a 5-card major, but I'd like to try to find a fit in the majors. Do you have a 4-card major?"

Choosing Diamonds

- When you have two 4-card minors, bid the diamonds.

- By bidding this way, most of the time, you will have 4 diamonds whenever you bid them. It's just an extra piece of information for your partner.

- Notice that this hand does not have a 4-card major. After your partner bids, you'll want to bid 1NT.

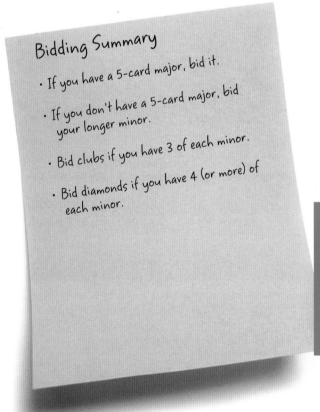

Bidding Summary
- If you have a 5-card major, bid it.
- If you don't have a 5-card major, bid your longer minor.
- Bid clubs if you have 3 of each minor.
- Bid diamonds if you have 4 (or more) of each minor.

RESPONDING TO A MINOR

If your partner bids a minor suit, you should answer with a major if you can

Before when we were talking about the bidding, we talked about trying to find an 8-card trump suit using both your hand and your partner's. If your partner bid a major, then she promised 5 in that suit and you only needed 3 to get to the 8-card fit.

When your partner bids a minor, however, she is now

saying, "I don't have a 5-card major, but I might have a 4-card major. Do you have a 4-card major?"

If you have a 4-card major, this is the opportunity to bid it. Notice that even if you only have 6 points, you can bid either major without leaving the one level—another reason that the minors are so "convenient."

A 4-Card Major

- Your partner bids 1 ♣, so you want to bid 1 ♠.

- Don't get fooled into supporting the club suit. She'll rebid them if that's where she wants to be.

- If she has four spades, she'll probably say 2 ♠.

- If not, she'll probably say 1NT.

Strong Hand

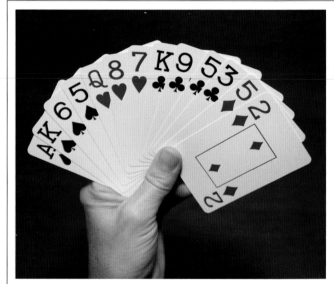

- This hand is the same shape as the last one, but this one has 13 points instead of 6.

- The bid is the same when you're responding to the minor. You say 1 ♠.

- You can show your points on your next bid, either by jumping to game in spades if she supports your spades or jumping to game in no trump.

38

If you and your partner have the same 4-card major, she will raise your suit. She'll bid on the two level with just a basic opening hand or jump to the three level with stronger points. If she has 20 points and a fit with you, she will jump all the way to game. In these examples, you found an 8-card fit that you might not have found without the convenient minor.

It also could be the case that you *don't* have matching 4-card majors. In that case, you and your partner will try to get to a no trump contract. In fact, at high levels of bridge, more contracts are played in no trump than they are in any of the four suits. The last resort would be to play in a minor. If your partner has a very unbalanced hand with a long minor suit, she will rebid her minor. This tells you that her original bid of 1 ♣ or 1 ♦ was actually referring to a real suit, and it wasn't part of the convention.

Longer than 4 Cards

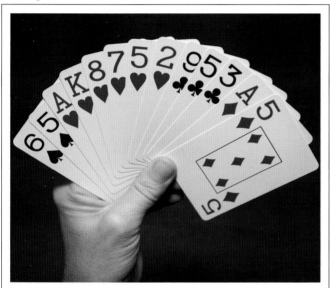

- In this hand you have six hearts.

- You still bid 1 ♥ in response to a minor.

- Now when your partner bids something else, you repeat your hearts.

Resist Temptation

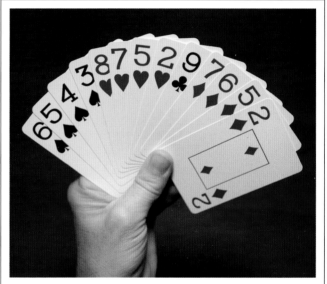

- Again, your partner has bid 1 ♣.

- This hand is terrible. Not only do you not have any points, but you are short in clubs! If you pass, she might end up in a 4-card trump suit.

- Even though you have two 4-card majors, keep quiet.

- If your hand is so weak, the opponents will probably be bidding anyway.

TRICKIER RESPONSES

It seems straightforward until you get a hand that doesn't fit the formula

What if you don't have a 4-card major when your partner bids his minor? That actually happens a lot. In that case, you're probably going to want to try no trump. Remember, no trump scores much higher than a minor, so it's an appealing contract as far as points are concerned.

The downside to no trump is that there is no way to stop

the opponents if they have a long suit. They can just keep playing their suit until they run out, and there's nothing you can do to stop them. If there's a trump suit, however, you can trump in as soon as you're out, rendering the opponent's suit powerless.

Because of this, many beginning players shy away from

No 4-Card Major

- Your partner bid a minor, but you have no 4-card major. How do you tell your partner no?

- You go to no trump. You have a few cards in every suit. You're balanced.

- Your partner will probably agree with it unless she has a wildly imbalanced hand.

Supporting the Minor

- In this case, your partner has bid 1 ♣.

- You technically could bid 1NT, but it's a little risky. You have only two little spades and two little hearts.

- A better bid is 2 ♣. You know your partner has at least three clubs, so you have the 8-card fit.

- When you have such a weak hand, you'd rather have the power of a trump suit.

playing the contract in no trump. Don't get into this bad habit. If you have a balanced hand—three or four in almost every suit—then you can feel comfortable going there. The opponents can't have too many.

On the flip side, you may find yourself with two majors—a much better situation than no majors! If you have four in both majors, you should go "up the ladder," which means start low and move up. In other words, bid the hearts, the lower suit. By bidding hearts first, it allows your partner to bid 1 ♠ when the bidding comes around to her.

•••••••••••••• GREEN ● LIGHT ••••••••••••••
If you have five spades, whether it's five spades and four hearts, or five spades and five hearts, then you should bid the spades first. It makes rebidding easier, and once you make that rebid, your partner will know that you have five spades because you chose NOT to go up the ladder.

Both Majors

- Your partner bid a minor, asking for your 4-card major.

- You have both majors, so you go "up the ladder" and bid 1 ♥.

- If your partner has four hearts, she'll say 2 ♥.

- If she has four spades, she'll say 1 ♠, which you then support.

Uneven Majors

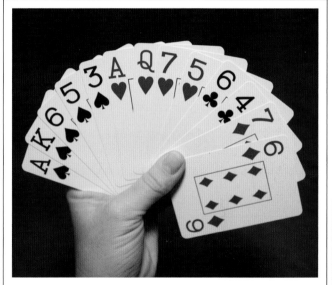

- In the previous hand, you went up the ladder.

- This time you have a longer spade suit than heart suit. In this case you would say your 5-card spade suit first.

- You can offer your hearts on the next bid.

- She'll know you have five spades because you would go up the ladder if you only had four.

RESPONDING WITH NO TRUMP
Your partner has bid a minor, but you don't have a 4-card major

Over a partner's bid of a minor, there are very specific point guidelines for the responder. First respond with a 4-card major. If you don't have one and have a fairly balanced hand, bid 1NT with 6 to 10 points, bid 2NT with 11 or 12 points, and bid 3NT if you have 13 to 16 points. If you have more points, you should be interested in slam, but we'll address slam bidding in a later chapter.

The upside to this bidding is that your partner (the opener) can be pretty confident in his next bid (or pass). He knows you have a balanced hand with no 4-card major, and he knows roughly how many points you have. The downside to this bidding is that the opponents also have all this information.

Another time to use the no trump bid is when the opponents interfere. Let's say you do have four spades. Your partner

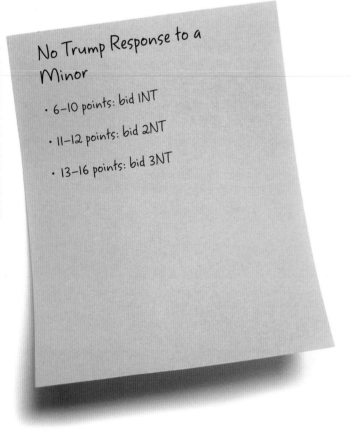

No Trump Response to a Minor

• 6–10 points: bid 1NT

• 11–12 points: bid 2NT

• 13–16 points: bid 3NT

Responding with No Trump

• Your partner bid 1 ♦.

• You don't have a 4-card major, but you do have a

balanced hand, and you have 12 points.

• Your bid is 2NT.

opens 1 ♣, and you're all set to say 1 ♠, but the opponents do it first! Now what? Now you can go to no trump—either 1, 2, or 3 depending on your point count.

If the opponents interfere between your partner's bid and your bid, but it's NOT your suit, be more careful about bidding no trump. Let's say your partner bid 1 ♦ and you were all set to say 1NT because you don't have a 4-card major. But before the bidding reached you, the opponent to your right jumped into the bidding with a bid of 1 ♥. Don't bid no trump unless you can stop the hearts, because that's the lead that you're

going to see from the defenders. If you don't have another good bid, just pass.

Jumping to Game

- Your partner bid 1 ♣.

- You don't have a 4-card major, but you do have a

- balanced hand and you have 14 points.

- Your bid is 3NT.

Retreating to No Trump

- Your partner bid 1 ♦.

- The next bidder said 1 ♥. He has five hearts, so you don't want to be bidding your heart suit anymore.

- But you're also not worried about the opponent's suit if you're in no trump.

- You have 11 points. Your bid is 2NT.

REBIDS

The opener has bid, the responder has responded, and now it's back to the opener

Opening bids aren't so hard, but the second bid can be tricky. It not only depends on what is in your hand, but it depends on what your partner responded and whether or not the opponents interfered.

If you open with a minor and your partner responds with a major, you first see if it's a fit. If you do have four, then your next bid will be in that suit. If you have the basic opening points, then you should just raise your partner to the two level. If you have 16 to 18 points, then jump to the three level. And if you have 19 or 20, then take a chance and jump to game.

But let's make it harder and assume you don't have a fit. If your partner responded with hearts, you can say 1 ♠. She

Rebidding a Minor

- Your first bid was 1 ♦, and your partner responded with 1NT, which implied 3 cards or fewer in both majors and a weak hand.

- In no trump, the opponents will take advantage of the fact that you only have (at most) four spades between you and you can't trump in.

- Rebidding your diamonds is a much safer bid than staying in 1NT.

Supporting the Responder

- The bidding has been 1 ♣ by you and 1 ♠ by your partner.

- You have 14 points and four spades.

- Ignore your beautiful six club suit. You want to be in a major.

- Raise your partner's bid to 2 ♠.

may have four hearts and four spades. If, however, she says a spade, there's not much point in saying the hearts. She skipped over them. She would have gone up the ladder if she had four. In this case, you would most likely bid no trump.

There is a chance that she has five spades and four hearts, which is why she skipped over the hearts, but in that case, she'll come back with the heart bid and you'll find your fit.

Finally, there may be a situation when you want to rebid your minor suit. While we prefer to be in a major or in no trump, sometimes it's better to fall back on the minors.

Bidding the Other Major

- You bid 1 ♣ and your partner responded with 1 ♥.

- You were hoping for 1 ♠. Go ahead and bid 1 ♠ yourself. Your partner may have four of each major.

Going to No Trump

- Except for 1 card, this hand is virtually identical to the previous one, but the 1 card makes a difference.

- You bid 1 ♣ and your partner responded with 1 ♠.

- You were hoping for 1 ♥. There's no point in bidding the hearts now because your partner skipped over them.

- Bid 1NT.

BACK TO THE MINOR

A few more details to make the convenient minor a little more complicated

Learning the convenient minor will take your game up a level, especially if you're interested in playing duplicate bridge. In rubber bridge, being in the higher scoring major is preferable, but not critical. In duplicate bridge, you rarely want to be in a minor. The convention helps you get to a bid in either the majors or in no trump.

A bridge teacher I know has a saying to discourage his students from bidding those minors. He likes to remind them that "diamonds are for weddings and clubs are for the golf course."

Beginning players struggle with *playing* no trump, so they tend to shy away from *bidding* no trump. They head back to the minors, because they find it easier to play with a trump

Rebidding a 5-Card Minor

- I've mentioned that I don't like to rebid a 5-card minor, but there are times when you might want to.

- Let's say the bidding went 1 ♦ by you, pass by the next two players, and 1 ♥ by the opponent to your right.

- No trump would be horrible with just 2 little cards in the opponent's suit.

- Rebidding diamonds here would be okay.

Two Minors

- This hand is so minor heavy that you know you'll probably end up there unless your partner can work some major magic.

- Bid 1 ♦ first. If your partner says anything but 3NT, bid your club suit next.

- This is better than rebidding your diamonds, because it shows that both your minors are real suits, not just short convenient minors.

suit. Don't fall into this trap! The solution would be to work on your no trump play. I mean think about it. Just because your playing isn't great yet, is that an excuse to make your bidding worse?

There are times, however, when you really don't have a choice. As hard as you try, you can't manufacture an 8-card fit in a major if you don't have it. And it's hard to go to no trump if the opponents are bidding a suit that you don't have. In these cases, you do have to play in a minor.

I've included some examples below where this is the case, but every time you're thinking about going back to the minor, you should ask yourself if you have a good no trump gamble instead.

Opening with No Trump

- If you have a really strong balanced hand, you can open the bid 1NT, rather than saying a minor.

- This implies 15 to 17 points and a balanced hand.

- This hand is a perfect example of a 1NT bid.

- The next chapter is all about opening 1NT.

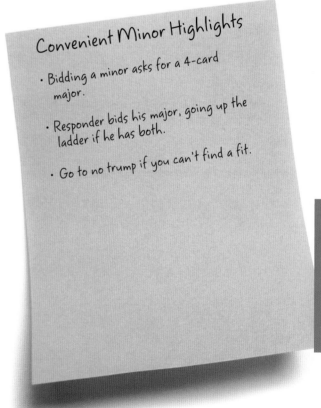

Convenient Minor Highlights

- Bidding a minor asks for a 4-card major.

- Responder bids his major, going up the ladder if he has both.

- Go to no trump if you can't find a fit.

OPENING 1 NO TRUMP
A balanced hand that has between 15 and 17 points should open 1 no trump

Sometimes you get a hand that just is screaming to be in no trump. You have tons of points and no long suit. Your gut tells you that maybe you should just start with no trump rather than do the convenient minor. Well, your gut would be right in this case, but opening no trump requires a very specific type of hand.

As you've learned, responding with 1NT implies a weak hand and no fit. Opening in 1NT is an entirely different animal. Not only are you starting at the top of the one level, but you're also telling your partner that you're okay with the "high card wins and no trumping in" kind of game. If you're okay with that, then you better have some high cards.

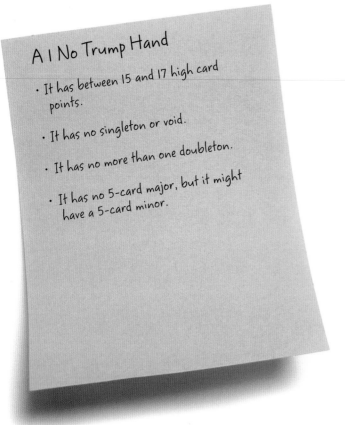

A 1 No Trump Hand

- It has between 15 and 17 high card points.

- It has no singleton or void.

- It has no more than one doubleton.

- It has no 5-card major, but it might have a 5-card minor.

No Trump Hand

- This is an ideal no trump hand.

- It has 17 points. It's perfectly balanced.

- Bidding 1NT is much better than bidding 1 of a minor because when your partner comes back with her 4-card major, you still won't have a fit.

To open a hand in 1NT, your high card points should add up to 15, 16, or 17. That's it. No more, no less. It might not make sense now, but by the end of this chapter you'll realize how helpful it is for your partner to know a very specific point count.

A no trump hand should be balanced. You need a few cards in every suit. You should never open 1NT with a void (no cards) or a singleton (1 card) in a suit. You also should avoid opening no trump when you have more than one doubleton (2 cards).

It's okay to bid 1NT and still have a 5-c[...]
remember, we'd rather be in no tru[...]
beginners are better off not bidding [...]
You don't have the tools at this poin[...]
fit unless you tell your partner you h[...]
the bat.

STATE [...]

Kath[...]
Educational Admin[...]
Center for [...]
Innovation in [...]

S101 Social and Beh[...]
Stony Brook, NY 11794-[...]
631-632-7696 Fax: 631-632-[...]
klusteg@erols.com
www.ceie.sunysb.edu/ceie

Five-Card Minor

- This is a good no trump opener.

- The hand has 16 points and is relatively balanced.

- It does have a 5-card diamond suit, but no trump is a better bid.

Two Doubletons

- This hand is not a good 1NT opener.

- This hand has 17 points, but it has two doubletons.

- Open this hand 1 ♦.

- If your partner says 1 ♥, then you should jump to 3 ♥ to show your points and your heart fit.

RESPONDING TO 1 NO TRUMP
What to say when your partner bids 1 no trump

One of the great things about bidding 1NT is that your opponents have to start on the two level if they want to interfere. Another great reason is that you've described your hand so well to your partner. And finally, the last great reason is that there are wonderful intricate responses developed by some fabulous bridge players that help you and your partner get to a perfect game—Stayman and transfers.

These are two conventions that I'll describe later in this chapter, but I'm not sure a beginning player should be worried about learning these bids right away. Once you feel comfortable with the basics of the game, however, then Stayman at least should be the first new gadget that you add. Both the Stayman and transfer bids will elevate your game tremendously.

0 to 7 Points

- Your partner has said 1NT.

- If you don't have a 5-card suit, you should pass.

- If you do have a 5-card or longer suit, bid it. Your partner's 1NT bid promises at least two in all suits. You have a weak hand and are better off playing with a trump suit.

- Bid 2 ♠ with this hand.

- This is a drop dead bid. She should pass.

8 or 9 Points

- Your partner has said 1NT.

- Pass with 8 points and a flat hand.

- Bid 2NT with 8 points and a 5-card suit.

- Bid 2NT with 9 points and a flat hand. That describes this hand.

50

I love these bids, and I like to think that you'll hang onto this book and use it to get you to the next level. I also hope that there are some people who already know how to play bridge but have picked up this book to update their bidding or to improve their game.

If you're a pure beginner, however, read these two pages and move on to Chapter 6. The game of bridge will give you plenty to remember and work on as it is.

10 to 14 Points

- Your partner has said 1NT.

- With a flat hand, bid 3NT, which is game. You know you have enough points because he's been so specific.

- With a 5-card suit, bid that suit on the *three* level. This bid for this hand would be 3 ♥.

- He will either go to 3NT if he only has two hearts or go to 4 of your suit if he has three or more.

15 or More Points

- Your partner has said 1NT.

- As with the 10- to 14-point hand, bid your suit on the three level if you have a 5-card suit.

- After your partner bids again, you need to look for slam. This will be explained more later.

- If you don't have a suit, start looking for slam in no trump right away.

BASIC STAYMAN
Learning the Stayman convention in response to a 1 no trump bid

The Stayman convention (named after Samuel Stayman) is probably the most widely used convention in bridge, and it is only used after your partner opens in no trump.

Stayman is similar to the convenient minor in that it is used to find a four-four fit in the majors. After your partner bids 1NT, you are going to bid 2 ♣. It will never be another suit. From here on out, your 2 ♣ bid will not say anything about your clubs. It's a question posed to your partner: "Partner, I have a 4-card major and at least 8 points, so do you have a 4-card major, too?"

If your partner does have a 4-card major, she will then say it. If she has *both* hearts and spades, she will say the hearts first, going up the ladder.

If your partner doesn't have a 4-card major, she will say 2 ♦.

Bidding Stayman

- Your partner has said 1NT.

- You have this hand. You don't have quite enough points to be in game in a minor, but you do for game in no trump or a major.

- You could bid 3NT, but you feel you might be better off in hearts if your partner has some hearts.

- This is why we love Stayman. Bid 2 ♣, and your partner will tell you if she has four hearts.

Responding to Stayman

- You opened 1NT, and your partner came back with 2 ♣.

- In this hand, you have four spades.

- Bid 2 ♠.

This says nothing about her diamonds. It may seem a little ridiculous not to just go back to no trump instead of bidding the diamonds, but the 2 ♦ denial bid will come in handy later as your bidding gets more advanced.

Do not use the Stayman convention if you don't have at least 8 points and at least one 4-card major, because you're promising both. If your partner doesn't have a 4-card major, you're going to end up back at 2NT, so you better have at least enough points to raise it up a level.

············· GREEN ● LIGHT ··············

Stayman can be used after a 2NT bid as well. If your partner opens 2NT, Stayman is the same, except that you say 3 ♣ and you can now use it with as few as 5 points.

Another Response

- You opened 1NT, and your partner came back with 2 ♣.

- In this hand, you have four spades and four hearts.

- Go up the ladder by starting with a 2 ♥ bid.

Denying a 4-Card Major

- You opened 1NT, and your partner came back with 2 ♣.

- She's asking for your 4-card major, but you don't have one.

- Bid 2 ♦. This says that you do not have a 4-card major.

OPENING 1 NO TRUMP

MORE STAYMAN

You learned the responses to Stayman, and now here are the responses to the response

You're probably thinking Stayman is pretty easy. Responding in 2 ♣ to ask for a 4-card major is pretty straightforward. But don't forget that you have to keep bidding.

If your partner came back with a major, and you also have 4 cards in that suit, repeat the suit. If you have only 8 or 9 points, repeat at the three level. You don't know if your partner has

15 points or 17 points. If she has the 17, you have enough points for game. If she only has 15, then you don't. By bidding at the three level, you are inviting her to game. It's up to her to look at her hand and decide whether or not to accept the invitation. If you have 10 to 14 points, bid the suit at the four level. You don't want to bid just 3 because she might pass. If

Inviting to Game

- Your partner bids 2 ♥, in response to your Stayman bid, telling you she has four hearts.

- You also have four hearts, so you have the 8-card fit you need. Bid 3 ♥ because

you can't quite get to game by yourself.

- She'll go to 4 ♥ if she's on the high end of her 1NT bid.

Going to Game

- Your partner bids 2 ♠, in response to your Stayman bid, telling you she has four spades.

- You have an 8-card fit, and between the two hands, you have plenty of points for game.

- Bid 4 spades.

you have more points, look for slam.

Now let's say you *don't* have a fit, either because your partner responded with diamonds or the other major. In this case, take it back to no trump. If you have 8 or 9 points, say 2NT. If you have 10 to 14 points, say 3NT. You do not want to say your suit. Your bid of 2 ♣ implied a 4-card major. If your partner has both majors and was just going up the ladder, she can take the bid back to spades.

Returning to No Trump

- Your partner bids 2 ♥, in response to your Stayman bid.

- That's not your 4-card major, so you're going back to no trump.

- Look at your points. Should it be 2NT or 3NT?

- Bid 3NT because you have 11 points, plenty for game.

- If your partner also has four spades, she will correct the contract and bid 4 ♠.

After a Diamond Response

- Your partner bids 2 ♦ in response to your 2 ♣ Stayman bid.

- She does not have a 4-card major, so you're going back to no trump.

- Look at your points. Will it be 2NT or 3NT?

- You only have 8 points, so bid 2NT and let your partner go to three if she has 17 points.

TRANSFERS
A new way to show a 5-card major after a 1 no trump bid

Stayman is a convention that is used for 4-card majors. It is always 2 ♣. Transfers are used when you have a 5-card or longer major. Notice I said major. Transfers are only used with major suits (although later on in your bridge career you may learn about minor suit transfers). The transfer bids are either 2 ♦ or 2 ♥. Nothing else.

The transfer bid gets its name from the fact that you are transferring your bid to your partner. You want the no trump opener (the big hand) to be the one who says the suit, not the one who actually has the suit. This keeps the hand with more points hidden from your opponents. Remember whoever declares the suit first is the one who will be the declarer and will play the hand.

In order to transfer, bid the suit *beneath* your major. For

Transfer to Spades

- Your partner has bid 1NT. You have five spades and 12 points.

- Before you learned transfers you would have said 3 ♠ with this hand.

- Now you want your partner to say spades, so you say the suit below spades. You say 2 ♥.

- Your partner will now say 2 ♠ when the bid comes around.

Transfer to Hearts

- Your partner has said 1NT. You know you have a fit in hearts, because she has to have at least two hearts in her hand.

- You want her to say the hearts though.

- You say the suit below hearts, so your bid is 2 ♦.

- Your partner will say 2 ♥ on her turn.

instance, if you have five or more hearts, you bid 2 ♦. If you have five or more spades, you bid 2 ♥. You always do this on the two level, no matter how many points you have. And once you play transfers you always play transfers. From here on out if your partner bids 1NT, diamonds will mean hearts and hearts will mean spades.

Your partner (the 1NT bidder) will be saying transfer and then, when it's her turn to bid again, she will bid the suit *above* the suit that you bid, *regardless of her support for that suit.*

Weak Hand

- This hand is so weak that you can't imagine bidding with it, but then your partner opens 1NT.

- Leaving her in no trump would be a disaster. At most, you have four hearts between you. The opponents have nine or more.

- You have to be in a trump suit. Bid 2 ♥, which is a transfer to spades.

Both Majors

- Your partner has bid 1NT.

- Even though you have five spades, you also have four hearts, so Stayman is a better bid than a transfer.

- Bid 2 ♣ with this hand.

- If your partner says 2 ♦, you can say 2 ♠, which would show five spades.

MORE TRANSFERS
Once you've transferred your suit to your partner, what's your next bid?

Transfers on the first round are easy. It's either 2 ♦ or 2 ♥. There's no other bid. Once you've made your partner say your suit, you have to figure out the next bid. This is a little harder.

The hands on this page are the exact same hands that were on the previous page, since the two bids go together.

The beauty of transfers is that you have a lot more wiggle room than you did with the old way of doing things. If you only have 3 points, but you know you should be in a suit, you can transfer the bid to your partner and then pass when it comes around to you again. Now your partner can't raise you. He accepts the transfer and you pass. By the time it gets back

Transfer to Spades

- Your partner said 2 ♠ at your request.

- You know you should be in game because you have 12 points, but which game? Spades or no trump? Do you have a fit or does he have only two spades?

- You should bid what you know. You know you should be in game, so bid the game, not the suit. Go to 3NT.

- Your partner knows you have five spades. He will go back to spades if he has three or more.

Transfer to Hearts

- Your partner bid 2 ♥ after you transferred.

- What do you know? You know you should be in hearts because your partner has at least two, but you don't know if you should be in game or not. It depends on your partner's points.

- Bid 3 ♥ but not the game. This tells your partner that you have six hearts. He'll pass or go to 4 ♥ if he has 17 points.

to him, there are three passes, so he can't bid.

If you have more points, the bid is good, too. With 8 or 9 points you can invite your partner to game. If you have 8 or 9 points after you transfer, you should make another bid. If you only have five in the suit, you should go back to no trump. You don't know if you have a fit. You also don't know if you have enough points for game. Your partner has to make both decisions, but it's a very informed decision.

If you have six in the suit but only 8 or 9 points, you bid 3 of your suit. You don't know if you have the points for game, but

you do know it should be in hearts because you definitely have the 8-card fit.

If you have game-going points (10 to 14), then the thing you know for sure is that you should be in game. Your next bid should either be game in your major (if you have six of them) or game in no trump (if you only have five in your major). If your partner has three or more in your suit, he can switch back to the major.

Weak Hand

- Your partner opened 1NT, and you realized that your hand is no help in no trump but it might be some help in a suit.

- Your first bid was 2 ♥, which transferred to spades when your partner bid 2 ♠.

- Now you pass.

- The beauty of this bid is that your partner can't get you in trouble. Without transfer bidding he could still raise your "drop dead" bid of 2 ♠ through misunderstanding.

Both Majors

- In this hand, you decide to bid Stayman rather than transfer by bidding 2 ♣.

- Your partner answers with 2 ♥. You jump to 4 ♥.

- You're quite happy when you discover that your partner only had two spades, so you made the lucky choice of bidding Stayman instead of transfer.

BASIC CARD PLAY
Enough with the bidding, let's play cards

Analyzing the Lead

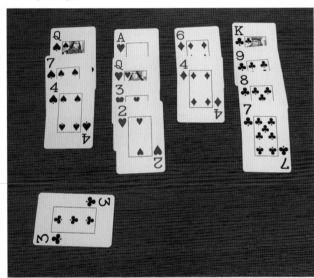

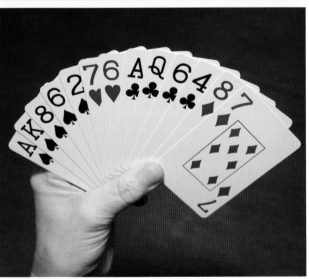

Once you've gotten through the challenge of bidding the hand, you're now faced with the daunting task of actually trying to achieve your contract (the bid you ended up with). Because the opponents get to lead the first card, that's where you should start your planning. As soon as the lead comes out, the dummy goes down on the table. You should take a minute or two to look at the dummy and look at your hand. Look at your trump suit. Is it solid? See what the problem suits are. See what your good suits are. Make a plan as to how you're going to play the hand.

Too often the lead comes down and beginner players just look at that suit. That suit is the opponent's suit. He chose it, not you. You should look at everything, find your advantages, and then think about how you're going to deal with the opponent's suit.

First, think about why he chose to lead that particular card.

- In this hand, the 3 of clubs was led by the opponents.

- You look at your hand and the dummy's hand. You have the ace, queen, and two little clubs, and the dummy has the king and three little clubs. Why would the opponent think that the club lead was a good one?

- In this case, you have a long club suit, so you can guess that the opponent is short in clubs. He was hoping that his partner had the ace.

- If so, the partner could take the trick and lead a club back for him to trump.

- So you should make sure that the opponents are out of trump before you go playing your nice high clubs.

- Win the trick in your hand and then start playing your trump suit.

Often you'll get a clue as to what is in his hand. For instance, the top of a sequence is considered a good bridge lead, so if a player leads the king of diamonds, you can assume that he also has the queen. That might be helpful if you have the jack.

A player might also lead a short suit, hoping he can get a trick by trumping in the next time the suit is played. Look at your hand and the dummy and see if you think this is likely. If you are short in that suit, it's probably not a short suit for the opponents. If you have some length though, it might be the case.

Once you've analyzed the lead, now you have to play a card from the dummy. Every hand is different, so there's no hard and fast rule, but if you have high cards in both the dummy and your hand, you will generally benefit by playing a low card from the dummy. Force your opponents to go high in the third hand and maybe you can capture something. Or, if they go low in the third hand, maybe you can get the trick cheaply.

- In this hand, the lead from the left hand opponent (LHO) was a 2 of hearts.

- Now it's dummy's turn to play. The ace is obviously the highest card, but you have the queen in your hand. What's the right move?

- This is a perfect example of playing a low card on the second hand.

- If your right hand opponent (RHO) has the king, she will now play it. She gets that trick, but you now have the next two when hearts are led.

- If your RHO does not have the king, your queen will beat anything she puts down. You might even win with your 10.

- On the other hand if you go up with your ace, your queen is vulnerable. It will fall on the king the next time hearts are played.

Second Hand Low

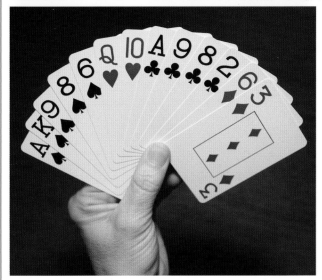

PULLING TRUMP

Don't let your opponents have a shot at using your most powerful tool

Pulling Trump

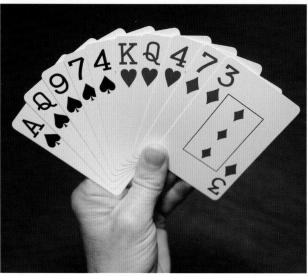

In the last section, I recommended that you get rid of any trump cards that the opponents may have before you start playing your high cards. This is referred to as "pulling trump," and it's a good habit to get into.

If you've bid correctly, you've ended up with at least 8 cards in the trump suit you've chosen. If you have 8, the opponents can only have 5. If you have 9, they only have 4. And so on. The more trump you have, the more advantages you have. And one of the biggest advantages you have is that you are able to "waste" a few of your trump in an effort to take away their trump.

Let's say hearts are trump and you are missing 4 of them. Even if they're little ones, they are still powerful enough to knock out your high cards in other suits. Because of that, the minute you get a chance to be on lead, you want to play trump. It their 4 trump are split 2-2, then you only need to

- The opponents took the first two tricks by playing their ace of clubs and their king of clubs. Then they led another club, which you took with your queen.

- Everyone followed suit on all three of those tricks. That means 12 clubs were played and your jack is the only club left.

- You're happy to have the card, but if you play it now, it will get trumped by one of your opponents.

- Because you have 9 trump cards—spades—they only have 4.

- Your strategy now should be to play spades, so they have to give up their four spades. This is called pulling trump.

- Once their trump is gone, you can play the jack of clubs. They will have to throw a heart or diamond, and you will throw a low diamond from your hand. The dummy hand will win the trick since your jack is good.

play trump twice before they have no more. Now you can play your high cards in the other suits without fear of the opponents trumping in.

Pulling trump is good even if you're missing the high trump. Many times beginner players will shy away from pulling trump because they don't have one of the top honors. (Honors are A, K, Q, J, 10.) Don't let that change your strategy. Avoiding the ace of trump is not going to make it go away. The ace of trump will always take a trick for your opponent, and he deserves to get a trick with it. But he doesn't deserve to get a trick with that other little trump that he also has in his hand. Pull it, even if it means you have to lose to the high one first.

- In this hand you have 9 trump between you, but you're missing both the ace and the king. The opponents have taken the first trick with the club ace.

- When you get the lead back, don't be afraid to pull trump. The opponents will take the ace and king spade tricks, but they were going to take them no matter what.

- Look at your hand and the dummy's. What other trump are you missing? You're missing the 6 and the 4. Do you want them to win tricks with the 6 and the 4 of trump?

- If they do, the opponents are taking *four* of your tricks rather than just the two. Keep pulling trump when you get the lead back.

Don't Be Afraid

COUNTING TRUMP
If you can't count all the cards, at least try to track the trump

Pulling the Last Trump

Counting cards may be illegal in a casino, but it's a critical part of bridge, and you might as well get in the habit right from the start. Eventually you're going to learn to count the cards in every suit, but for right now, focus on counting the cards in the trump suit.

This is why. When you pull trump, you want to only play the suit as long as you need to. You want to hold on to the rest of your trump so you can use them to stop the opponents when they play suits you're short in. So how do you know when they're out of trump? The answer is you have to count the cards.

There are two different methods for counting trump. Both are equally valid, but some people's brains work better one way and other brains prefer the other way. Basically, you either add or subtract.

In the first method (adding), you count the cards as they

- In this hand, spades are trump, and you have pulled two rounds of trump after taking the first trick.

- Both opponents followed suit both times.

- You know your opponents only have one trump card left.

- Many players wonder if they should use two of their trump to pull just one of the opponent's trump.

- Here's a good rule of thumb: If the trump that's out is the highest trump left, don't pull it. If it's a lower one, go ahead and take it.

- There are exceptions to every rule, and no where is that more true than in bridge. See the next hand for a time when you would choose not to pull that last trump.

come out. In the first trick, if everyone follows suit, you have four. In the second trick if everyone follows suit, you're now up to eight. You then add what's in your hand and what's left in the dummy. If you get to 13, you're done. If you don't, you have to do it again.

In the other method, you only count the opponents' trump cards. You start with what's in your hand and in the dummy. Add that together and subtract from 13. You'll get a number—let's say it's 5. That's how many the opponents have. So you play a round of trump and both opponents follow suit. That's two—remember you're counting just the opponents' cards. Subtract that from five. You have three left to pull. Pull again, and keep counting.

- Spades are trump; you've pulled two rounds of trump after taking the ace of diamonds on the first trick.

- They still have a little trump left, but you want to use the two trump in the dummy before you pull that last one.

- Play the ace of clubs in your hand. That gets rid of the club in the dummy, freeing you to trump clubs.

- You lead a low club. Trump it in the dummy. Lead with a low heart from the dummy back to your hand, taking the trick with the ace of hearts. Lead the last club in your hand; trump it with the last trump in the dummy.

- Come back to your hand using a low heart and taking the trick with the king of hearts in your hand.

- *Now* you pull the last trump. If you'd pulled it earlier, you would have used up one of the trumps in the dummy that you needed.

Using the Trump

TOSSING YOUR LOSERS
Set up a long suit in one hand and you can dump the losers in the other

Side Suit

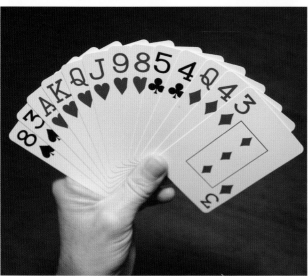

Sometimes you get lucky and you get two long suits between you and your partner. Occasionally you even know this from the bidding before you see the dummy come down.

Let's say your partner opens her diamond suit. You respond with your heart suit and she rebids her diamonds. You know now that she has a real diamond suit, and you have support for it. But you also have six hearts, and she thinks you only have four. You rebid your hearts, and she supports them. Now you have a fit in hearts and a fit in diamonds. This is called a "double fit," and it's great news. You choose hearts for the trump suit, because that's the major and you'll get more points, but the diamonds will pay off in the play. Look at the hand and dummy below. See how beneficial the long diamond suit will be. You can get rid of all your low spades.

This diamond suit is often referred to as a "side suit." When you have a long side suit, pulling trump is more important

- Your contract is 4 ♥, which means hearts are trump, and you have to win 10 tricks. In other words you can only lose 3 tricks.

- The lead was the 5 of diamonds.

- You suspect that the diamond lead came out because it was a singleton.

- Why else would they lead a suit that was so good for you? And your partner was bidding that suit, so it was no surprise.

- What's your plan of attack?

- Your black suits are terrible. You need to discard the ones in your hand on the long diamond suit in dummy.

- Your plan is to pull the trump and then run the diamond suit.

than ever. If you have 9 cards in your side suit, how many do the opponent's have? Only 4. Let's say they don't split evenly—which is actually the more likely outcome—so that one player has 3 and the other has only 1. You can play 1 round of diamonds and that's it before they trump in. Take away their trump and you can run your diamonds all day long.

- This hand is the same as the previous one, but now you're 6 tricks into the game.

- You've played the ace and king of hearts, which pulled all their trump.

- Then you played the queen, king, and ace of diamonds, which left you in the dummy with no more diamonds left in any of the other three hands.

- Now you're playing another diamond from dummy. When it gets to your hand, you throw one of your loser spades.

- You're out of diamonds, so you could trump, but there's no need because the diamonds are all high. Toss a loser instead of trumping.

Running the Suit

SIDE SUIT TRICKS
Learn some guidelines to effectively run a long suit

Bad Transportation

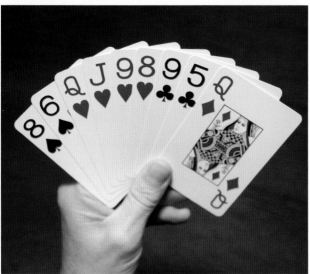

The examples on the previous page showed the value of a long suit. If no one else has that suit, even the littlest cards in that suit will be good.

In that example it was especially easy to run the long suit because you had all three of the top honors. However, the declarer could easily have messed up that hand if she played those high cards in a different order. Remember that the hand that wins the trick is the one who leads to the next trick. She had to make sure that she ended up in the dummy in order to continue to play the diamonds.

The best way to do this is to take your winners on the short side first. Then lead over to the winners on the long side. In that example, the declarer should win with the queen first and then lead a little one over to the ace.

Look at the pictures here to see what happens if you don't. You get trapped in the wrong hand. In bridge terms, you've

- The declarer first pulled trump, and then it was time to run the diamond suit.

- When you have a long suit, take your winners on the short side first, but the declarer for this hand misplayed it.

- Do you see her problem?

- All she has left in her hand is the queen of diamonds. If she plays that, she'll win it and all the diamonds will be good, but how does she get over to the dummy to lead them?

- If she had ended up in the dummy, she could have thrown away her losing clubs or spades. Now she's stuck in her hand and will have to lead with them.

messed up your transportation. Sometimes you have a nice solid suit to run, but you are missing some of the top ones. Don't let this stop you. Running the suit is still valuable. You just have to take one or two losses before that can happen.

If you happen to be short in the suit in your hand, it's even better. You can win tricks with trump while you're waiting for your long suit to set up.

- In this hand, spades are trump and you win the first lead of a club with the ace in your hand.

- You do have a long side suit in dummy's hearts, but they're so low, will they ever do you any good?

- The answer is yes, as long as you have a good split.

- First pull trump. Then play two heart tricks—one that your ace of hearts wins and one that you cede to the opponents. Hopefully eight hearts have fallen in this effort.

- You have three more in dummy, and the opponents have the other two.

- Let's say they lead a diamond now. Win it in the dummy and play another heart. The two high hearts fall, but you trump them in your hand and now your little hearts are set up.

Setting up a Suit

FIRST & THIRD

When you have two hands to play from, how do you choose which one to lead?

If you're the declarer, you have two hands to work with—your own and the dummy's. It would be easy if you had ace, king, and queen all in one suit, but inevitably you don't. Usually you're missing a few honors. So how do you play a suit when you're missing some of the high cards?

The best thing for you is to have the opponents on lead.

If they're on lead, you're playing the second card and the fourth card. You will almost always benefit by playing low on the second card and seeing what high card comes out on the third. But since you will be winning most of the tricks (you hope), most of the time you will be on lead and not the opponents. You have to figure out which hand is going

King and Queen

- In this hand you have the king and queen in your hand and nothing in the dummy.

- Start the spades in the dummy. Lead a two.

- If the ace is on your right, you've set up your king

- and your queen to be good without using either one of them.

- If it's on your left, it doesn't matter which way you play it.

Ace and Queen

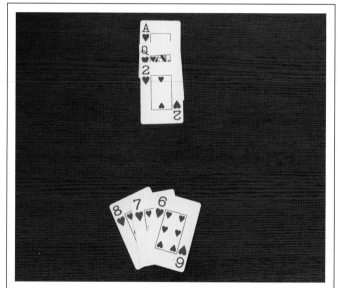

- In the heart suit, you are missing the king.

- In the dummy you have both the ace and the queen.

- You want to make the dummy the third hand.

- Lead a low heart. If the king comes out, cover it with the ace. If a low card comes out, then stick in the queen and gamble.

to play the first card and which hand to is going to play the third card.

The general rule is to lead from weakness toward strength. So if you have a suit that has an ace and a queen in the same hand and nothing in the other hand, you want to start with the "nothing" hand and lead toward the hand with the strength.

Another way to look at it is to lead *toward* the card that is underneath the card you are missing—in other words, make that one the *third* card. So if you're missing the king, the

queen should be in the third hand. If you're missing the ace, the king should be in the third hand. And so on.

The reason for this is that you're hoping the missing card is in the "second" hand. If they go "high" and play it, then you haven't wasted an honor. If they go "low" and wait to see what you do, then you win the trick.

Another Ace and Queen

- In the diamond suit, you are also missing the king, but this one is a little different. You have one honor in each hand.

- What is the card *beneath* the missing card?

- The missing card is the king, and the card beneath it is the queen. The hand that holds the queen then (the dummy in this case) should be third.

- Lead low from your hand toward the dummy.

Let the Opponents Lead

- In this hand you have an honor in each hand. Which way do you lead?

- The answer is you don't if you can help it.

- If you lead this suit, the opponents will capture one

of your honors. You will inevitably have to lose two clubs.

- If they lead it, however, you make both your king and queen good by going low on the second hand.

COUNT YOUR WINNERS
Playing a game in no trump requires a different strategy

Count the Winners

Let's say you've ended up in a 3NT contract. This is game, so you're happy about that, but it also means that you and your partner haven't been successful in finding a trump suit. If the opponents have a great suit, they can run it and there's nothing you can do to stop them.

Against a no trump contract, the most common lead is fourth down from the longest and strongest suit. So, right off the bat, you know which suit is best for the opponents (or at least your left hand opponent). File this piece of information away in your brain.

Now, before you play a single card, study your hand and the board. Count the winners in each suit when your two hands are combined. By winners, I mean the *sure* winners—the tricks you can take without losing the lead. Let's say you have the king, queen, jack, and 10 in your hand as you do in the diamond suit below. These are "likely" winners. But you

- Let's count the winners in these two hands.

- You have two in spades, one in hearts, three in clubs and zero in diamonds.

- That comes to six winners, and you need nine, since the contract is 3NT.

- Where are you going to get your other winners? Clearly from your diamond suit.

- That's the suit you should play first.

have to lose a trick to the ace before they become winners. They are therefore not "sure" winners.

Let's assume your count of sure winners is less than the number of tricks you need to make your contract. Now you have to figure out how you're going to get your extra tricks.

There are a number of ways to get your extra tricks: setting up a long side suit, getting rid of a top honor to set up "likely" tricks, and finessing to name a few. We'll go over these in more detail throughout this chapter.

If you've figured out which suit is going to give you your extra tricks, you've also then figured out what suit to play first.

- For this hand, the contract is 1NT. Believe it or not, this contract is generally harder to make than 3NT.

- Count your winners. There are three winners—two hearts and a diamond.

- You need four more.

- Where are they likely to come from? Don't get fooled into thinking that your spade king is a likely one. If the ace is on the wrong side, you get nothing in spades.

- Your extra tricks will probably come again from your long diamonds.

A Harder Hand

LOSING THE LEAD

In no trump you want to lose a few in order to win a few

Lose the Lead

When I teach no trump, the hardest thing to impart to my beginning students is the idea of losing the lead.

First, I guess it's somewhat counterintuitive to give away a trick when the goal is to take as many as possible. Second, so many of them have tried a no trump contract and gotten burned badly when the opponents started running their suit. What they don't realize is that the reason they've been burned is because they waited too long to lose the lead.

As we discussed on the previous page, after you count your sure winners, you stop to figure out where your potential winners are. By definition if they're not sure winners, they are going to require that you either take a gamble that you might lose the lead (called a "finesse" in the bridge world) or you deliberately lose the lead in order to set up a long suit.

Don't be afraid of losing the lead, as long as you do it early, while you still have a way to stop them from running their

- In this hand, you have six winners: two spades, three hearts, and one diamond.

- When asked, many beginners would say that hearts was their best suit.

- But you only have four hearts and the opponents have nine hearts. Hearts is *their* best suit, which is why they led it.

- Your best suit is clubs, even though you're missing the ace and king.

- Your strategy is to win the first heart but then play a club, even though you're losing the lead.

- They will win and lead a heart again. You "stop" the hearts with the king this time.

- Play another club and lose the lead again. They win with the other club honor. If they lead yet another heart, you still have it stopped and now your clubs are good.

suits. A card in the opponents' suit is called a "stopper" for that very reason. The more stoppers you have the better, but you have to hang on to them for them to work. Of course, there's always an exception. Occasionally the dummy comes down and you see that not only can you make your contract with sure winners, but you and your partner are completely vulnerable in one suit. You breathe a sigh of relief that they didn't find it on the lead. Now might be the time to take your money and run.

Don't Use Your Stoppers!

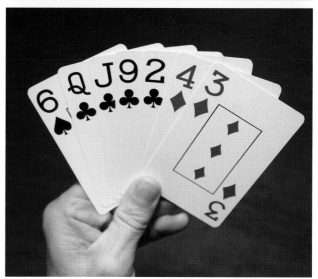

- Now let's see what happens if you took your winners right away.

- This is the same hand on the previous page, but in this hand the 6 stoppers have been taken before the clubs are set up.

- Now your hand doesn't look so great does it?

- You still have to lose the lead to get your remaining tricks. That dilemma didn't go away.

- But now when you lose the lead, they can lead back just about anything and you can't stop them.

- You can be pretty sure they're not going to lead your club suit.

75

LONG SUIT PLAY

Setting up a long suit is your easiest route to success in no trump play

Run a Suit

Sometimes you find yourself in a no trump contract, but you have a long minor suit that works out brilliantly in your no trump play.

Because I'm a big fan of duplicate bridge, almost all of the bidding I'm teaching you in this book is designed to help you have success when you're playing duplicate. The strategies for success in rubber bridge can be slightly different. Remember that in duplicate, your goal is to get the highest score possible.

Because of that you often choose to be in a no trump contract when you and your partner have a nice long minor suit fit. Tricks in a no trump game score higher, so you need fewer tricks to get the same or more points.

This long minor suit, however, is still your key to success. Again, when your opponent leads and the dummy comes down, you want to count your winners. Think what a solid

- The contract is 6NT.

- In this hand you have a solid club suit in the dummy's hand. You only have one club in your hand, but that's enough to help out.

- Because you have seven clubs, the opponents only have six. Unless there is the highly unlikely split of six in one hand and none in the other, you can count on all six of the dummy's clubs as sure winners.

- The nice thing about this long suit is that you can throw your three loser spades and a loser diamond on the clubs in the dummy.

- Once you're done running clubs, lose the king of hearts. That's the one trick you have to lose and the rest of your cards are good.

6-card suit will do! That's six winners right off the top. Look at the first example. This contract is in 6NT, which is a small slam. They're missing quite a few high cards, but it just doesn't matter because the club suit is so helpful.

In the second example, the suit is long but it's not solid. The length of the suit should be an immediate signal to you that you should start playing that suit immediately, even though you'll probably lose the first trick.

If you're having trouble visualizing the entire play of the hand from just one picture, take a deck of cards and set up the hand exactly as you see it in these pictures. Now play it out. This should make it really clear to you.

- The contract is 3NT.

- The player on your left led a heart, which you won with your queen. That's one trick.

- Count the rest of your winners. You have the heart ace and the ace and king of spades. That's it. Just three more, which added to the first trick makes a total of 4 tricks.

- Where are the other 5 tricks coming from?

- The answer is clearly from dummy's six-club suit.

- It is imperative to play a club and get rid of the ace, before you take any of your sure winners.

- The opponents will win. Now, if they lead another heart, you have your ace. If they lead a spade, you have your ace. If they lead a diamond, you might have to wait a round to win, but then you can run your clubs.

Set up a Suit

77

DANGER SUITS
How to avoid getting hurt by the opponents' long suit

Dangerous Opponent

The hardest thing about playing no trump is that you have no magic card to stop the opponents from running their long suit. Instead, you have to have a high card (or two or three!) in their suit.

In the first example, you bid 1 ♦, your partner says 1 ♥. She clearly has at least four hearts—your weak suit—and since everything else is covered, you say 1NT. Your partner also has an opening hand, so she says 3NT. But then the dummy comes down, and look at the 4-card heart suit. Ugh. It doesn't have a stopper! This is your danger suit.

The key in this particular case is to make sure that when you lose the lead to set up a suit, you ensure that your left hand opponent (LHO) is the one who wins it. That way if she leads a heart, your king is going to be good—either that trick or the next heart trick—no matter who holds the ace. If your right hand opponent (RHO) leads the heart though, you are

- The contract is 3NT. You've won the first trick with the heart queen.

- Counting your winners, you realize that you have only 8 of the 9 tricks you need.

- Where is your ninth trick coming from? The diamonds, once you lose the queen.

- However, your heart suit is looking pretty scary. If your RHO gets on lead, he can play a low heart and trap

your king. Your RHO is your dangerous opponent.

- Your only safe bet is to put your LHO on lead.

- Play a low diamond from your hand up to the king. Now play a low diamond from the dummy to your 10.

- Ideally the queen will be sitting with your RHO, but even if your LHO has it, he can't do damage with a heart lead.

trapped if the LHO holds the ace. Sometimes you have an ace in your weak suit, but you still need to recognize that it's your weak suit and know how to protect yourself against a run by your opponents. The second example shows how you can do this.

If one player has the long suit, you can try to avoid letting her get the lead, but if her partner can lead the suit to her, it doesn't matter. So the key is to let them play a few rounds in that suit to drain the partner of her cards. Once you're sure the partner is out, you can take your winner. Now she can't lead that suit if she gets the lead.

Drain the Partner

- Your LHO opened something called a "weak 2" bid, which you'll learn about later. So you know that he has six spades in his hand.

- Your partner doubled and you risked a 3NT bid because you have a spade stopper.

- But you only have the one stopper. This is important.

- The lead is obviously a spade. When the dummy comes down, you count that the LHO has six, you have four, and the dummy has one. How many does that leave for the RHO? Just two.

- Don't play the ace right away. Let the LHO lead the spades again. Now play it.

- Now you can take the club finesse. Even if the RHO does have the club king, he won't be able to lead a spade back.

THE FINESSE

Learn how to take a gamble when you're missing a top card

Ace and Queen in One Hand

The finesse is one of the hardest things for beginners to learn, but also one of the most critical. Work hard to grasp the concept.

To begin with, you have to understand that a finesse is a gamble. You're missing one of the top honors, and you don't know which of the defenders has it. Sometimes the bidding will help give you a clue, but usually you're flying blind.

While you can finesse for any card, I'm going to talk about finessing for the king to simplify the process. When I talk about finessing for the king, it means that you hold the ace and queen, but the opponents have the king. Believe it or not, if the finesse works, the opponents won't ever win their king.

If the ace and queen are in one hand, make that the third hand. Begin the trick from the opposite hand.

If the king happens to be in the second hand, this person has a dilemma. If he plays the king, you will take it with your

- In this hand you have the ace, queen, and jack of spades in the dummy.

- Lead a low card from your hand.

- The player to your left will probably play a low card.

- Play the queen from the dummy.

- If the fourth player doesn't take the trick, you know that the person on your left has the king.

- Now come back to your hand with the ace of diamonds.

- Play a low spade again and this time put in your jack.

- See how nicely the suit worked for you?

ace. If he doesn't play the king, you can take the trick with your queen. Most players in the second seat will play a low card, hoping you'll go up with your ace anyway. Don't! This is the moment of the finesse. Put in the queen.

I know that it's unclear whether this second player has the king or not. The low card doesn't tell you anything. But that's the gamble. Sometimes that player will have the king and sometimes the player in the fourth seat will have it and take your king. So it goes.

Here's what you have to realize: If you don't take the gamble, the opponents will win their king no matter what. Right? You go up with your ace instead of taking the gamble. What's the next highest card? It's the king. Whenever you lead that suit again, the king will win no matter where it's sitting.

- In this hand, you are also missing the king of spades, but this time the ace is in the dummy and the queen is in your hand.

- If you just have those two honor cards, then you can't technically do a finesse, but there's still an appropriate way to play the suit.

- Start the play in dummy and hope the king is on your right.

- If you have QJ10, however, as you do in the club suit, you can do a finesse in a different way. Start in your hand and play out the queen.

- Presumably your left hand opponent will play a low card.

- Do not go up with the ace. Play the 2.

- You're still in your hand. Now lead the jack of clubs. Keep doing this until his king drops and then cover it with the ace.

Ace and Queen in Opposite Hands

OTHER FINESSE TIPS

Finessing for the queen and other thoughts about finessing

Finessing Both Ways

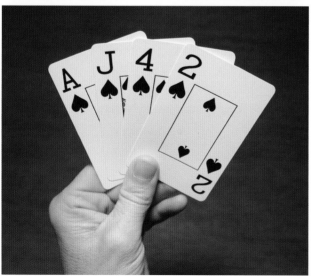

The finesse tactics are slightly different when you're finessing for the queen. To begin with, if you have enough cards in your suit, you may not even have to finesse. If you have 9 cards in a suit between you and the dummy, then the opponents only have 4. You can take the chance that the cards are split 2 and 2. If they are, then play out your ace and then your king, and the queen will fall on the second trick. If they're split 3 and 1, you'll still benefit if the 1 is a singleton queen.

If you only have 8 cards, however, the odds favor trying the finesse, because it's a lot less likely that the queen will drop. Some players like the phrase "eight ever, nine never" to help them remember when to take the queen finesse and when to go for the drop.

When you're missing the queen, you occasionally have the ability to take the finesse in either direction. Because both the ace and king can cover the queen, you might be able to

---

- In this hand, the suit you want to set up is your spade suit. You have 8 cards, which means the opponents only have 5.

- But you're missing the queen. You have the ace and jack in your hand and the king and 10 in the dummy.

- If you guess right, you might make all your spades good.

- Are there any clues in the bidding?

- Your left hand opponent bid 1 ♦. Your right hand opponent (RHO) passed. It's not much to go on, but the person who bid is more likely to have the points.

- Plan to finesse through the dummy. Start in your hand with the 2 of spades.

choose which one to lead up to. See the photos on this page for a good example of this.

Of course then you not only have to know how to take a finesse, you have to know how to choose which way to take the finesse. Don't worry if this is beyond your grasp right now. It will come. Look for clues in the bidding. Maybe one defender is obviously short in a suit. Maybe it's clear that one defender has all the points. Use what you can from the bidding to help guide your play.

One final tip: If you are missing both the king and the queen, finesse twice. Odds are with you that they're not in the same hand. The second example on this page shows you how this would work.

- In this hand, you have a nice diamond suit, but while you have length, you are missing the king and the queen.

- The odds are against both of them being in the same hand, so you want to finesse the same way twice. One of the times should work.

- Start with a low card in the dummy. If your RHO goes up with the king or queen, cover it with the ace.

- If she doesn't—which is the more likely scenario—put in the jack.

- Let's assume it loses.

- Whatever the opponents lead back, win in the dummy. Now lead a low diamond to the 10 in your hand.

- This time you hope it works. Now play your ace, and your diamonds are set up.

Finesse Twice

THE BEST LEADS

Every hand is different, but there are some leads that are always appealing

Now that all the declarers have learned how to play, it's time to teach the defenders how to play. One of the most common mistakes beginning bridge players make is to assume that if they lose in the bidding, their job is done for that hand. They see it as the declarer's hand to win or lose. While this is quite often a big piece of the picture, the defenders have a huge role to play as well. Defense is 50 percent of the play, and good defense can really affect the outcome of a contract. It all begins with the opening lead.

If you and your partner have been active in the bidding, your lead becomes much easier. You know what your partner's strong suit is, and perhaps she knows what yours is.

Your Partner Bids

- Your partner bid hearts during the bidding, so you are going to lead hearts.

- You only have two hearts, so lead your high one first—the 4.

- A high card then a low card will show your partner that you have only two.

You Both Bid

- During the auction, you both bid. You bid clubs, and your partner bid a heart.

- Lead your partner's suit. When he gets in, he will lead your suit.

- In this case, lead a low heart.

Maybe it's the same suit. Either way, you should lead to your partner's strength.

But if you haven't been bidding, there are other leads that are equally as good. Your best bet is to look for a sequence of touching honors: AK, AKQ, KQ, KQJ, QJ, QJ10. Leading the top card of one of the sequences is a great lead. First of all, you send a message to your partner that you have the card beneath it. Second of all, you're setting up those lower cards to be good the next time the suit is played.

If you don't have a sequence, look for a singleton, which

means only 1 card in a suit. If you lead that you will become void in that suit. The next time the suit is played, you will be able to trump in. Hopefully that will happen before all your trump are pulled.

Some players lead a doubleton for the same reason, but this rarely pays off and other leads will generally be better for you.

Top of a Sequence

- In this hand you have an ace and a king in hearts. This is an excellent lead.

- Play out the ace of hearts. This gives you a chance to look at the dummy, before making the next lead.

- You may or may not want to play out your king.

Singleton

- In this hand, you want to lead your singleton 4 of clubs.

- If your partner has the ace and leads clubs back to you, you can trump it.

- Even if your partner doesn't have the ace, he may be able to get the lead before all your trump are pulled.

THE BIDDING HELPS
Listen to the bidding to get a clue to your best possible lead

If bridge were an easy game, you'd always have one of those great leads to make, but it's not an easy game, so leading tends to be a challenge more often than not.

During the bidding you obviously were paying attention to what your partner was bidding, but were you also paying attention to what the opponents were bidding? That might be a clue for you. Let's say their bidding went 1 ♣,

1 ♥, 1 ♠, 2 ♠. Which suit wasn't mentioned? It's diamonds, of course. If a suit isn't mentioned by the opponents, it usually because they don't have the suit. But the cards didn't disappear. Somebody has to have the suit, especially if you don't have much in that suit either. It's probably your partner, and that means that it's probably the best suit for you to lead. You want to lead toward strength.

Bidding Clues

- All the bidding was done by the opponents.

- It went 1 ♦, 1 ♥, 2 ♣, 2 ♥, 3 ♥.

- What suit wasn't bid? Spades.

- You should lead a low spade.

Choose the Major

- This bidding went 1NT and then 3NT by the partner.

- You have two good suits here, the hearts and the clubs.

- They would have tried to get to a major if either one had one, so that's where they are vulnerable.

- Lead the heart suit.

Or maybe the bidding went 1NT and then 3NT. There were a number of ways that either bidder could have talked about a major if they had one, but since they both shied away from it, then perhaps they are vulnerable in the majors. Choose hearts or spades as the suit you're going to lead.

Another thing to consider is what suit the dummy bid. If the player to your left was bidding hearts, but the contract ended up in clubs with the player to your right as declarer, then you know that the declarer doesn't have much in the heart department. They would obviously choose hearts over a minor.

You may choose in this case to lead a heart, knowing that the declarer will probably have to play high on the second hand. That way you're not going to be trapping any high card that your partner might have.

More Bidding Clues

- This time the bidding went 1 ♣, 1 ♠, 2 ♣, 2 ♠, 4 ♠.

- There are two unbid suits here, but you also have some other information.

- You know that the opening bidder has a long club suit. You also have a long club suit.

- Maybe your partner has a singleton or void and can trump. Lead a low club.

Lead Through Strength

- In this one, they bid all four suits, so it's hard to guess which one might be a strength for your side.

- If you can't find a good suit to lead, then you should lead through strength.

- In this hand, the dummy bid spades and clubs. Lead one of those suits.

BAD LEADS
There are some leads that are just a plain bad idea

Now let's see if we can narrow the lead possibilities even further, because much of leading strategy is knowing what NOT to lead as much as knowing what you should lead.

From years of watching my beginner bridge players, I know there will be a few of you out there who will feel compelled to lead out the highest card in your hand. Playing a high card is only good if it's the top of a sequence of high cards. It's

a terrible idea if it's the only honor card in the suit. If it's an ace, you won't capture anything with it, and if it's not the ace, you've just given your highest card to the opponent.

If you have an ace in a suit, it's a suit that you want led to you. If you have an ace in a suit, go to a different suit entirely for your lead. You don't want to bang out that ace, but you also don't want to underlead it either, in case the declarer is

Process of Elimination

- The easiest way to pick your lead is to use the process of elimination. Which suits do you want to avoid?

- You're playing against a 4 ♥ contract, so you hearts will not do you any good.

- Clubs and spades each have an ace. Wait to use those.

- Diamonds are left. Lead a low diamond.

Another Example

- In this case, spades are trump.

- You have an ace in hearts. Don't lead that suit.

- You have broken strength in diamonds, so don't lead that suit.

- Clubs are left. You have nothing in that suit. Lead the top card.

sitting there with a king that you might have captured if the suit was led to you.

If you have an honor card in the suit, then you should lead a low card to find out if your partner also has one, perhaps even the ace. If she does have the ace, then she'll win it and lead a low card back to your high card.

But even that has a caveat. If you have only 2 cards in a suit (called a doubleton), and one of them is an honor, go to a different suit. You still don't want to bang out that honor card, but this time you don't want to lead low from it either.

Leading Trump

- Many beginners think it's a disaster to lead trump, but experts lead trump quite often.

- Sometimes it's led to reduce the trumping opportunities if the bidding has indicated that is going to happen.

- Other times it's led because there are no other good leads.

- In this hand, hearts are trump, and there are no good leads in the other suits. Lead trump.

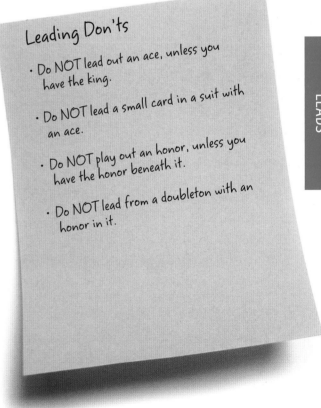

Leading Don'ts

- Do NOT lead out an ace, unless you have the king.

- Do NOT lead a small card in a suit with an ace.

- Do NOT play out an honor, unless you have the honor beneath it.

- Do NOT lead from a doubleton with an honor in it.

THE RIGHT CARD

You picked the suit, but now you have to pick the card within the suit

We've discussed strategies for choosing the right suit. Now you have to choose the right card within the right suit.

If you have a sequence you know you should lead the top card. You also know that you should never lead out an honor unless you have the one directly under it. So that narrows it down a bit. But let's say you have a suit with a queen, a nine, a five, and a two. All experts would agree that you can't lead out the queen, but which of the other cards is the best lead? The answer is that it doesn't really matter as long as you and your partner are on the same page. I can find three good players, one each who would stand behind one of those cards as the best lead.

Bottom of Something

- In this hand, spades are trump, so you can narrow the suit choice down to just hearts.

- Do you have something with a face in hearts?

- Yes, the jack. So, then you want to lead from the bottom of the suit.

- The lead would be the 3 of hearts.

Top of Nothing

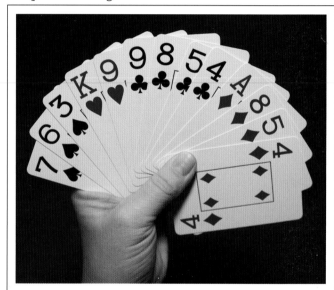

- In this hand, you've narrowed the suit to clubs.

- Do you have something with a face in this club suit?

- No. So you lead the top of this suit. You lead the 9 of clubs.

The method I'm going to teach you I think is the easiest one to remember, because it has an easily remembered acronym to go with it: BOSTON. BOSTON stands for Bottom of Something, Top of Nothing.

And in this case "Something" means "something with a face." Aces don't have faces, and neither do 10s, 9s, 8s, etc.

So, in our previous example of Q952, you would say, "Is there something with a face in this suit? Yes. The queen. Therefore, I'm going to lead the Bottom of Something, and the bottom is the 2.

Now let's say you had a suit with a 9753. Do you have something with a face in this suit? No, you have nothing in this suit. So, in this suit, lead the top. Top of nothing. Simple, right?

As I mentioned, the key is communication with your partner. If you play BOSTON, then your partner should play BOSTON. Your partner needs to know that if he sees a 2 come out of your hand, that it means you have an honor in that suit.

Many Choices

- In this hand, the bidding went 1 ♠, 2 ♠, so spades are trump and there are no bidding clues to go by.

- None of the other three suits looks especially appealing, but none is terrible either.

- You have these choices: 9 of diamonds (top of nothing) or 2 of hearts or 4 of clubs (bottoms of something).

No Good Lead

- These strategies will help you most of the time, but sometimes you get stuck with no good lead.

- If hearts are trump, this is a perfectly good example of no good lead.

- Many times I lead trump when I have no good lead, but you have a natural trump trick with the queen, so it's bad too.

- In this case, take your pick. They're all bad.

AGAINST NO TRUMP
The best lead to set up your long suit

The great thing about no trump is that the strategy is exactly the same for the defense as it is for the declarer. You want to figure out what the best suit is for either you or your partner and get rid of the opponent's stoppers in that suit.

Just as with the declarer, it's your long suits that tend to be the best suit to set up, not necessarily the suit with the highest cards in it. So identify your longest and strongest suit. This is the suit you're going to lead.

The best way to do that is to lead low in that suit. Most players lead fourth down from the top card. While that may seem somewhat arbitrary now, it will help out later when your skills become more advanced.

Sometimes you'll have two suits to choose from, so there are other factors that you'll need to rely on to help you choose.

Fourth Down

- In this hand, your best suit is pretty obvious. It's spades.

- You have both the ace and the king, but don't play them out just yet.

- Lead the fourth down, which is the 6.

- The next time you get in, there's a good chance you can take all the rest of the spades.

Two Choices

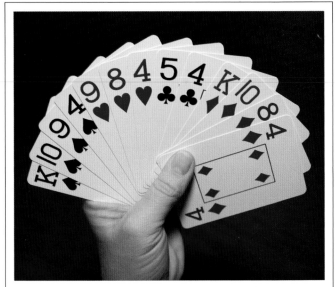

- In this hand, you have two 4-card suits, and they're both pretty equal.

- What was the bidding?

- It was 1 ♦, then 1 ♥, then 1NT.

- Since someone mentioned diamonds and no one mentioned the spades, choose the spades.

- The 4 of spades is your lead.

Pay attention to what your partner has bid and lead that suit to her. Or if your partner has led a suit to you, think about why she might have done that. Does she have a singleton? Does she have an honor in that suit?

Pay attention to what your partner has played. Is her nine winning the trick? If so, then you don't need to trump. Did she lead out a king? Lead that suit back so she can get her queen. Did she show out in a suit that last round? Lead that suit so she can trump it.

Work with your partner to set the contract. Think about what might be in her hand and don't become so enamored with your hand that you can't find the best defense for the partnership.

Wait and See

- Again, you're the second hand to play.

- Again, you should think about what your partner has.

- You have the ace of hearts, so you know you could win the trick, but the dummy's highest card is a 10.

- Don't play your ace. Hopefully your partner can take the trick.

Lead to Your Partner

- In this hand your partner bid spades, but the opponents stole the bid back and are in four hearts.

- Your spades are pretty crummy, but you still want to lead them, because they're your partner's strong suit.

- You can lead or tell your partner about your diamonds later.

SECOND & THIRD
Wait to see what your partner might have

When you can't see what your partner has, it's hard to know what to play—especially when you're new to the game. More advanced players can extrapolate from the bidding, leads, and a few tricks and figure out exactly what their partner has, but newer players are mostly playing a guessing game.

To cut down on bad guesses, commit this rule of thumb to memory: Second hand low. Third hand high.

If the opponent plays out an ace, obviously you would put a low card on it, but what if he plays a 4? You are only the second hand to play, so you should still play a low card. Your partnership always has two chances to win this trick. Let your partner be the one to win it this time. If you go high in the second hand, then you enable the declarer to play a low card from both his hand and the dummy and not lose a thing. If

Second Hand Low

- A small spade was played. You have the ace of spades and two little ones.

- You should go low here. See what your partner has.

- Even if the opponent wins, now he's put you in the fourth hand position, and maybe you can capture something with that ace.

Exception

- In this hand a low spade was led, and dummy's highest card is a jack.

- You only have two spades, the queen and a little one.

- In this case, you should probably go up with the queen, even in the second seat.

- If you go low, then your queen might fall on the ace or king next time spades are played.

you go low on the second hand, then the opponent has to play a relatively high card in the third hand to avoid giving you the trick too cheaply.

If, however, you're the third hand to play, you have to go high for exactly that reason. Let's say your partner played a 3 and the second card was a 2. If you play another low card, you're letting the opponents win with the next lowest card. You need to go high to force the declarer to play high. You might lose the trick, but maybe you're setting something up for your partner. She led it after all. Second hand low, third

hand high is not going to be a guideline to follow 100 percent of the time. Sometimes you might want to save a high card to cover a high card in the dummy. Sometimes going low would make your hand vulnerable. But in general, it's good bridge sense.

Third Hand High

- In this hand, your partner led the 3, the 6 was played in the dummy, and now it's your turn.

- You have the queen and the 9. Play the queen even though it's likely that the declarer has the ace.

- Maybe your partner has the king and the jack and would be thrilled to see those 2 cards drop.

Watch the Dummy

- If you pay attention to the cards in the dummy, you may not have to go as high as you think.

- Your partner played the 8 of clubs. The dummy played the 2.

- The dummy has the 9, 10, and queen. You have the jack and the king.

- You can play low on this hand because the declarer can only beat the 8 with an ace.

USE THE DUMMY
Noticing what's available in the dummy can direct your play

Seeing the dummy mostly helps the declarer, but the defenders can use that knowledge to help them as well. You now know half of what the opponents have and you know exactly where it is.

If the dummy is to your right, you're in great shape. Lead its weakest suit, the one with the fewest high cards. Declarer is going to have to play high on the second hand, which is

either going to let your partner capture something or it will protect your partner by letting her throw a low card on the third hand. If the declarer doesn't play high on the second hand, then your partner will have an easy time beating the dummy's weak suit.

If the dummy is to your left, it's a little harder. You generally want to lead through strength, and it's especially nice if

Use the Dummy

- Now that the dummy is down, and 3 tricks have been taken, you can make a more informed lead.

- Because you have five clubs and the dummy has five clubs, there's a good chance your partner might be short.

- Play out your ace. You can never trap the king anyway, and then lead a low one.

Other Strategies

- If you know from the bidding that the declarer rather than your partner is going to be short in clubs, then you'll have to come up with a different lead.

- Because the dummy is short in diamonds, you might want to lead a trump so the declarer can't use those trump on her low diamonds.

there's broken strength, such as an ace/queen combination or a king/jack combination. Your partner may have the missing card and the declarer just might take the gamble.

You also want to take a good hard look at the dummy if you're playing the second or third card to make sure that you aren't playing any higher than you have to. If you're playing the third card and dummy has the fourth card, see how low you can go and still win the trick. What's the highest card the dummy has? Can you just go one higher?

The Weak Suit

- This dummy makes leading easy.

- Since the dummy is on the right, you should pick the dummy's weakest suit.

- That is clearly clubs. Because you have the jack and 10, lead the top of your sequence.

Process of Elimination

- Even if you didn't have the obvious club suit lead, the other suits should direct you there.

- The hearts would be bad, because if your partner has the king, you would trap it between the ace and the queen.

- The diamonds are bad because you have the ace and the king is on the board. You want that suit led to you.

101

BREAKING A SUIT
Don't start a new suit if you don't have to

Believe it or not, when you're on lead, you frequently are providing a service to the opponent. If you have a nice sequence, then you're not giving anything away, but other than that, you're probably setting up the opponent's suit, giving them a free finesse, or trapping your partner's high card. It's so depressing.

Look at the first example. By leading a low card away from

your king of spades, the declarer gets a free finesse. She doesn't have to gamble any more, because her hand is the fourth hand. If she led the suit instead, you would have been fourth seat and her queen would have been captured by your king. The next two pictures give other examples of this.

As you can see, the lead frequently gives a gift to the declarer. So how do you minimize this? To begin with, you

Free Finesse

- You led a low card away from your king.

- The declarer played low in the dummy, and your partner put on the jack.

- The declarer won it with his queen.

- If you hadn't led the suit, he probably would have tried to finesse.

Setting up Cards

- In this hand, a low heart was led. The declarer could play low in the dummy because she had the queen in her hand.

- When the defense went up with the ace, both her high cards were set up.

- If she'd led the suit, the king would have been captured by the ace.

choose one of the good leads, like the top of a sequence or a singleton. These don't give things away. Of course, you don't always have that option, which brings us to the second part of leading strategy: force the declarer to lead a suit.

If she leads the suit, you benefit. Don't keep switching suits every time you get the lead. That's called "breaking a suit," and both sides generally prefer to have the other one break the suit. Stick with one that's already been broken, even if you know it might be void in one hand.

Trapping Your Partner

- In this hand, by leading a diamond, you trapped your partner's king.

- Sometimes, it may seem that all leads are a disaster, but it's not true, though they do frequently pay off for the other team.

- Be careful not to break a suit if you have another option.

Slough and Ruff

- If you know or suspect that the opponents are both out of a suit, then it is actually better to lead a different suit rather than continue.

- If you lead a suit that the opponents are both out of, the declarer can choose which hand to trump with and which hand to toss the loser, like they did in this case.

DEFENSIVE PLAY

SIGNAL FOR A SUIT
Your first discard is a chance to tell your partner which suit to lead

In just about every hand you play there's going to be a moment when you can't follow suit and you can't (or don't want to) trump, and you must throw a discard. Don't waste this opportunity. Every moment in bridge should be used if possible to further your goal of setting the contract.

The first discard should be a signal. You should be able to tell your partner what suit you want led the next time he gets

in. There are numerous systems that people use to signal their partner. You don't have to learn the most complicated system, but you should insist that your discards mean something, and you and your partner should get on the same page.

Many beginners start by discarding a card in the suit that they want led to them. The upside to this method is that it's

A High Spade

- You're out of hearts when hearts were led.

- In this hand, you definitely want spades to be led to you.

- Play the 8 of spades, which is considered a high spade.

- You could also play the 2 of diamonds, which would discourage the diamond lead.

A Low Heart

- A club lead would be great because the ace is on the board. So if they duck, you win, or if they take it with the ace, then you win the next time.

- But you can't throw your 7 of clubs, because it leaves your king vulnerable. If you tossed the protecting 7, the king would fall on the ace if the declarer didn't duck.

- Throw a small heart, which says you don't want hearts.

really easy to remember: If I want a spade, I'll toss a spade. The downside is that it's really limiting. What if you don't have a spade to spare?

Because of that, virtually all bridge players adopt a more complex discarding system. The most common discard system is called "standard" discarding. If you play a low card in a suit, you don't want your partner to lead that suit. If you play a high card in a suit, then you do want your partner to lead that suit. I recommend learning this system right off the bat rather than the simpler one mentioned above.

Against No Trump

- Standard discarding is especially helpful against no trump.

- In no trump, you're trying to set up a long suit. If you have to throw away one of the cards in that suit, then it's defeating the purpose.

- Throw a low card in a different suit.

- In this hand, you would throw a low club.

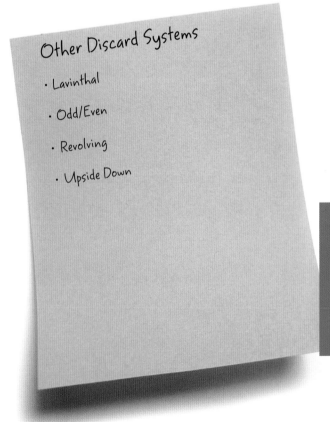

Other Discard Systems

- Lavinthal

- Odd/Even

- Revolving

- Upside Down

HIGH/LOW
Telling your partner that you have a doubleton can be handy

You can't talk while you're playing bridge, but you can make the cards talk for you, depending on how you play them. Giving your partner some knowledge of how many cards you have in a suit can be enormously helpful. The best way to start learning about giving count is to practice going high and then low when you have a doubleton. As you advance in bridge, you'll be able to convey lots of information about your

hand, but here's an easy way to start off down this path.

If you have 2 cards in your suit, you should play the highest one first. The next time the suit is played, you obviously play the low one. Now your partner knows that you had exactly 2 cards in that suit. He can look at his hand and look at the dummy and figure out exactly how many cards the declarer has in that suit.

High Low

- In this hand your partner has led the ace of spades

- You have two spades.

- Play the 3.

- You might not think it matters because the 2 and 3 are both low and pathetic, but when your partner next sees the 2, he'll know you're out.

Queen Doubleton

- The queen doubleton is the only exception to this high/low rule.

- Play the low card. If your partner continues with the king, your queen will fall and your partner will know it's a doubleton.

- That way you can put the queen on the ace only when it's a singleton or when you have the jack. Both show a way to get to your hand.

For instance, let's say that your partner plays the ace of hearts, and you have two hearts: the 10 and the 4. On the ace, put the 10. Now your partner plays the king, and you put on the 4. So eight hearts have been played. Your partner has two more little hearts in his hand. The board has two hearts as well. Who has the missing heart? Because you played high and then low, your partner knows for sure that the declarer has the missing heart. Now your partner can lead one of his little hearts, and you can use a trump to win the trick.

Let's say you had three hearts instead: the 10, 7, and 4. This time you put the 4 on the ace and the 7 on the king. Because your cards went from low to high, your partner will know that you have another heart in your hand. He's not going to lead the heart, because he knows that it's the declarer who can trump in, and not you.

Ace Doubleton

- Your partner led the king of spades, which promises the queen.

- Hold your breath and over-take the king with your ace.

- Now lead the low spade back to his queen.

- Now he can lead another spade for you to trump.

- If you don't, and he leads a spade to your ace, you're now stuck in your hand.

Three Cards

- Your partner has led the ace of spades.

- You have three spades. Play the 4 in this case.

- Next time your partner plays the spades, you'll play the 6.

- He'll know you have three spades, not just two.

THE PENALTY DOUBLE
If you think you'll set the opponents, you should double

Remember when I said there were fifteen words you can use in bridge? The other two words are "double" and "redouble."

The double was initially put in the bridge rules to inhibit players from bidding way over their capabilities in order to keep the opponents out of a game contract. For instance, if you and your partner were going to make a game in spades in duplicate bridge, you would get 420 points. In essence,

that means the opponents receive -420 points. So, if the opponents are only going to lose 50 points per trick, they can go down 8 tricks (8x50 = 400) and still get a better score.

Looking at the scores below, you can see how the penalty double makes a difference. Now they can go down 2 tricks and still have a better score, but the third trick makes it a bad bid. If someone is clearly stealing the bid from you and your

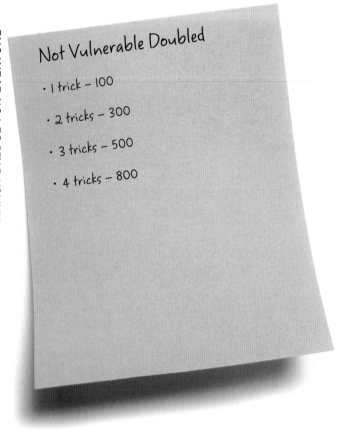

Not Vulnerable Doubled

• 1 trick – 100

• 2 tricks – 300

• 3 tricks – 500

• 4 tricks – 800

Double or Rebid?

- In this case, you and your partner had a clear 4 ♠ bid, and then the opponents stole it at 5 ♥.

- Do you bid 5 ♠ and go down? That's going to get you a bottom board if everyone else was allowed to play in 4 ♠.

- Your best bet is to double. If you set them by three, you've come out ahead of the pack.

partner, make sure you double!

You may also want to double if they get in over their head. Maybe they're not trying to steal the bid, but maybe they got up too high before finding their fit. Or maybe they don't have a fit. Or maybe you have lots of their trump. These are other good times to double for penalty.

Don't double indiscriminately, however, because if the opponents make their bid, then they get double the points instead of you getting double the points. They also get an extra 50 points, just for the insult of being doubled. And if they were not in game—let's say they were at three hearts—and their doubled bid makes, they've now reaching game without bidding. It was going to be 90 points (3x30), but now it's 90 doubled, which is 180 and over 100, so they get the game bonus.

And they might "redouble" and get quadruple the points.

Vulnerable Doubled

- 1 trick – 200
- 2 tricks – 500
- 3 tricks – 800
- 4 tricks – 1,100

Trump Imbalance

- In this hand, the opponents have bid 4 ♥, which you just love!

- They have eight hearts between them. But you have five hearts and know your partner has a void in hearts.

- Not only do you have all those hearts, but you have some extra points.

- This is a good time to double the opponents. You will most likely set them.

THE TAKEOUT DOUBLE
Use the double to mean something entirely different

It didn't take the top players long to realize that the *double* was a drastically underused word. Could they possibly use the double in some way that could convey a different meaning, other than penalty, and could they do it in a way that their partner wouldn't be confused and mistake it for a penalty double? The answers were yes and yes, and the takeout double was born. Now the double bid is used all the time.

Let's say the opponents bid 1 ♠, and while you have 13 points, you have only one spade, four hearts, four clubs, and four diamonds. What do you bid here? First of all, you have to start on the two level without knowing how many points your partner has. And which suit to pick? You'd obviously like the other major, but what if your partner only has two hearts but she has six clubs? Even though it's a minor, you'd much

The Bidding Box Cards

- If you're bidding with the bidding boxes, then the red card with the X on it is the double card.

- The blue card with XX on it is the redouble card.

- Players would like to use redouble more often, too, but it can't be used on its own. It can only be used following a double.

Classic Double

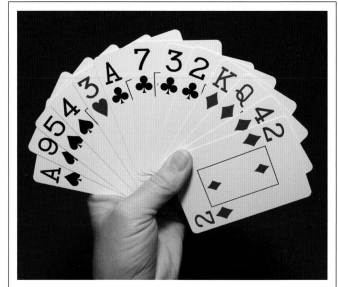

- The opponents have bid 1 ♥.

- You have one heart and four in every other suit.

- Double. This tells your partner that you are short in hearts, have points, and can support anything else he comes back with.

rather be in the clubs, but you might never find it. If you bid 2 ♥ and she only has 6 points, she'll probably leave you there in that terrible fit.

Enter the takeout double. If the opponents have bid, you can now legally use the double. A double at the lower levels (most players use it up to 3 ♠) means "take me out of the opponents' suit, partner. I have opening points, but I don't have a suit to bid. I'm short in their suit, so therefore I can support anything you say!"

So if the opponents bid 1 ♠, a double by your partner says,

"Bid anything but spades." If the opponents bid 1 ♦, a double would mean "bid anything but diamonds." In other words, "Take me out of their suit." Hence the name. Easy, right?

A Pretty Good Double

- Again, the opponents have bid 1 ♥.

- This isn't quite as perfect as the previous example, but it's still an excellent double.

- Don't get fooled into bidding 1NT because you have so many points.

- You'll be killed in the hearts without a trump suit. Double, once again telling your partner about your points and your short hearts.

Another Example

- Here the opponents have bid 1 ♠.

- You do have a suit to bid—the clubs—but double is a better choice.

- By doubling, you may find the heart fit.

RESPONDING
What to answer when your partner bids a takeout double

When your partner bids a takeout double, she's asking you to bid your best suit. But, like everything else in the game of bridge, the responses are a little more involved than that.

The first thing you need to know is that this bid is a demand bid. You can't pass, even if you have a Yarborough. (A Yarborough is a hand without even a single honor card.) If you pass, then the opponents are also going to pass and the double

reverts to its original intent of a penalty double. Remember, your partner was just using the double to convey a message. She doesn't actually want the double left in as the last bid. You are off the hook, however, if the player in between your partner and you bids. If he bids, then you can choose whether to bid or not based on your points and your suit holding.

But let's assume that the opponent didn't bid. Because you

Show Your Points

- The bidding so far: 1 ♥ by the opponent and a double by your partner. The next player passed, so it's your turn.

- In this hand you have 4 points. You still have to bid.

- You bid 2 ♣. After a takeout double, you are allowed to change suits on the two level. It does not imply 10 points.

When You Have Two Suits

- The bidding has been the same in this hand: 1 ♥, double, pass.

- You have two good suits here: four spades and five clubs.

- Choose the spades, because they are the major, even though the clubs are longer.

- Don't bid 1 ♠. Bid 2 ♠ to show 10 or more points.

have to bid even with 0 points, you need a way to show a higher point count. What I recommend is to make your bid at the cheapest possible level with 0 to 9 points and skip a level with 10 or more

Your obligation is to pick your best suit. This means your longest suit, not the suit with the most honor cards. Obviously, you also would choose a major over a minor. If your longest suit is the opponent's suit, then choose a different suit if you have one or bid no trump to show that you have that suit and no other suit to bid.

When You Don't Have a Suit

- Again, the bidding has gone 1 ♥, double, pass.

- Your best suit is the hearts.

- You don't have another suit to offer.

- Bid 1NT. This shows your partner that you have the hearts covered and fewer than 10 points.

Opponents Interfere

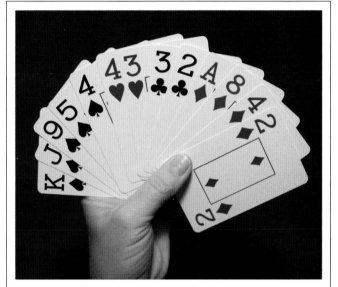

- In this hand, the bidding has gone 1 ♥, double, 2 ♥.

- You are off the hook. You don't have to bid.

- However, you do have 8 points, and you do have five spades.

- Bid 2 ♠. This is not jumping a level, but it is a free bid, not a demand bid, so your partner can pinpoint your points to 6 to 9.

BAD TAKEOUT DOUBLES
Times when you should just keep your mouth shut

Beginning players generally fall into two categories when it comes to the takeout double. There are those (the majority) who learn it and then forget that it even exists. Yet they are then tortured when they are unable to use the convenient minor because the opponents have bid. Inevitably, they end up bidding a 4-card suit and getting themselves into trouble.

The other types are the double abusers. They are the ones who use the double indiscriminately, when they clearly should either be passing or making a different bid entirely. There are very specific guidelines for a takeout double—listed on the Post-it note below—and very good reasons behind them.

You have to have opening points. Because you don't have a

Not Enough Points

- After a 1 ♥ bid, this hand has a perfect double shape, but not enough points.

- Double is not a good bid, because you're forcing your partner to bid, even if she has 0 points.

- And she's going to be counting on you for opening points, so she might bid too high.

Bad Shape

- The opponents have bid 1 ♥.

- You have 14 points, but hearts are your suit.

- Just pass. They're going to have some difficulty wherever they end up.

strong suit, you should at least have strong points. Even if you have the perfect shape for a double, you should pass if you don't have the points. The only time you might use a takeout double when you don't have enough points is after you've already passed. This way your partner will know that you're just being competitive.

You also have to be short in the opponents' suit. If you are, then by definition, you'll either have a suit of your own to bid or you'll be able to support any other suit. If, instead, you double when you have length in the opponent's suit, then you're almost guaranteed not to find an 8-card fit with your partner. Better to just pass and play defense. Let the opponents struggle to find the fit.

A Good Major Suit

- The opponents bid 1 ♠, and you're void in their suit.

- Technically, you could bid double here, but you might never find your heart fit, because your partner will never suspect that you have five of them.

- Bid your hearts. If they bid 2 ♠, you can double the second time around.

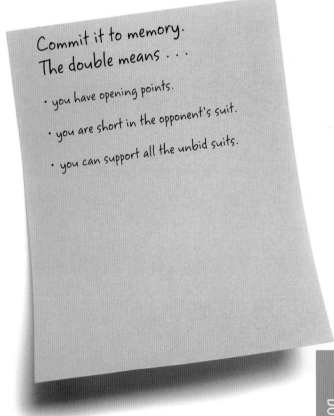

Commit it to memory.
The double means . . .

- you have opening points.

- you are short in the opponent's suit.

- you can support all the unbid suits.

OTHER EXAMPLES
Here are a few more scenarios where the double might come in handy

The double can come in very handy in many more situations. Once you become an experienced bridge player, you can add a variety of extra doubles to your repertoire. When I play 24 hands at either a tournament or at a club, I'd guess that in at least 10 of the hands we find that one of the four players uses the double card. At the same time, it's probably the

most underused card (bid) by inexperienced players.

One reason I love it is that it's a forcing bid. There aren't many forcing bids by an overcaller (the player after the bidder), so if you really need to know something about your partner's hand, you now have a way to make her bid. Keep in mind that you should only double for this reason if you have lots of

Lots of Points

- The dealer bid 1 ♦.

- Because the dealer has 13 points, and you have 19 points, there aren't many points left.

- If you bid 1 ♥, your partner might pass.

- Double to find out more about her hand. Then you can bid the hearts.

With Fewer Points

- In this case, you bid first, and you passed. Then the opponents bid 1 ♦ and 1 ♠.

- Your partner knows you don't have an opener, so you can feel free to double

here—showing clubs and hearts—without misleading her.

- The opponents may bid before it gets to her, but at least she'll know something about your hand.

116

points (17 or more.) The first example shows when you might want to use it for this reason.

It also can be used to keep the bidding low. It talks about several suits at once, so you can find out what works best for your partner without using up bidding space to describe your hand. This is especially handy when you don't have the points to do much bidding. See the second example.

And finally, it's handy when you want to keep your partner bidding, but you don't have a great bid. The fourth example shows that.

With Interference

- In this one, you started the bidding with 1 ♦.

- Your partner said 1 ♠, which only promises 4.

- You were all set to bid 1NT when the player on your right said 1 heart. Now you're not so comfortable in 1NT.

- Double in this situation. Your partner can rebid her spades, mention clubs, or go back to your diamonds.

To Find a Major

- The opponent bid 1 ♦.

- You do have a 5-card club suit to mention, but if you bid 2 ♣, you might never find a fit in the majors.

- Double instead. Yes, you might end up in a 7-card heart fit, but it's still a worthy gamble.

THE NEGATIVE DOUBLE

A more advanced use of the double and an exceptionally valuable one

The negative double is a double made in response to your partner's bid of a minor. When your partner has opened a minor, she is most likely looking for your 4-card (or longer) major. When you bid your major, your partner knows that you have at least four of that major but she does not know whether you have just four or more than four.

However, when the opponents make a bid of a major in between you and your partner, you have an opportunity. If you have five of the other major, then go ahead and bid it. If you have only four of the major, use the negative double instead.

For example, look at the first two hands below. They're

Four of the Other Major

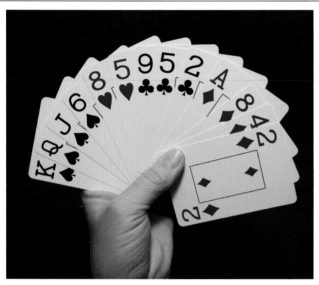

- Your partner bid 1 ♣.

- With this hand, you would say 1 ♠, and your partner would not know whether you had four or five spades.

- If, however, your RHO interferes and says 1 ♥, then you have an opportunity to be specific.

- You would double, which shows exactly four.

Five of the Other Major

- Again, your partner has bid 1 ♣, and the opponent has said 1 ♥.

- Now you bid 1 ♠. Your partner knows you must have five spades, not four, because if you had four you would have doubled.

- If there's no interference, you would just say 1 ♠ and your partner would not know you had five.

118

almost exactly the same, except for the number of spades. That makes all the difference. Let's say your partner bid 1 ♣, your right hand opponent (RHO) bid 1 ♥, and now it's up to you. Before you learned the negative double, you would have bid 1 ♠ with both these hands, and your partner would never know whether you had four spades or five spades. Now that you know the negative double, you double in the first example, because you only have four, and you bid 1 ♠ in the second example, because you have five.

If the opponents interfere with the other minor, then the double shows both majors, either 4 and 4 or possibly 5 and 4. Look at the third example. Your partner bid 1 ♣, your RHO overcalled 1 ♦. The negative double in this case would show both majors.

The negative double also helps you bid if you're shy of points. Look at the last example. The bidding went 1 ♣, 1 ♠. You'd like to say 2 ♥, because you have five of them, but you don't have the points. You should use the negative double here as well. It doesn't show that you have five, but at least your partner knows you have the hearts.

Both Majors

- Your partner has bid 1 ♣.

- If there's no interference, you would bid the hearts first—go up the ladder.

- But if your RHO says any of the other suits, you double.

- If he says a major, you double for four of the other major. If he says diamonds, you double for both majors.

Not Enough Points

- This is probably the most confusing use of the negative double, but it's a good one, too.

- Your partner has bid 1 ♣. Your RHO interfered with a 1 ♠ bid.

- You desperately want to bid 2 ♥ to show your five hearts, but that's a forcing bid and implies 10 or more points, so you can't.

- But you can double. It doesn't show five, but at least it shows four of them.

119

THE WEAK TWOS
Jump into the bidding even though you don't have the points

Every once in a while you'll get a hand that is just screaming to be opened, even though it doesn't have the requisite 13 points. Instead it has a great trump suit. Imagine if you had the ace, king, queen, and three little spades, but that's it in your hand, so you only have 9 points—only 9 points, but it's still six spades, including the top three. It seems a shame not to try to win the bid and make spades trump, right? If spades

are trump, it's pretty likely that your hand can take six tricks. If something else is trump, you might only get one before someone else is out of spades and trumps in. This hand is much better on offense than defense.

It didn't take much for bridge players to realize that they needed a mechanism to show a hand like this. The weak two bid was born.

Classic Weak Two

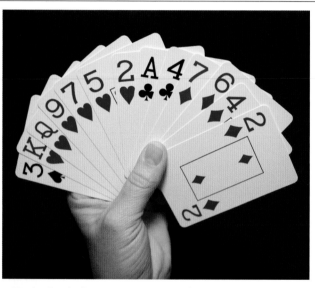

- You're the dealer.

- You have six hearts and 9 points.

- Your hand is too weak to open 1 ♥, but you feel that this hand is too strong to just pass.

- Bid 2 ♥ to show your partner that you have a nice suit but not many points.

Weak Two after a Bid

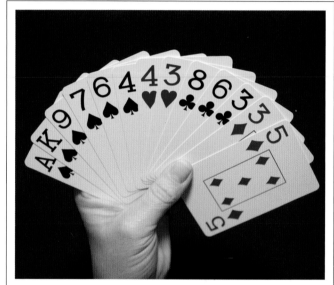

- Your right hand opponent (RHO) bid 1 ♣.

- You should bid 2 ♠. It describes your hand perfectly. You have 5 to 10 points and six spades.

- It also takes up a lot of bidding space, because it doesn't allow the responder to bid on the one or two level.

When you bid, you begin on the one level—1 ♠, 1 ♥, 1 ♦, 1 ♣, 1NT. Even if you're very strong, you don't start higher because you need bidding room to find the best suit for you and your partner. So if a player opens his hand on the two level, you should realize immediately that something unusual is going on. A bid of 2 ♠, 2 ♥, or 2 ♦ can be translated into "I have 6 cards in this suit, but my hand is too weak to open normally. I have between 5 and 10 high card points." (The bids for 2 ♣ and 2NT will be discussed in later chapters).

You don't mind taking up all this bidding room, because you don't need to poke around and find your suit. You're telling your partner that your hand is pretty decent as long as this is your suit. It stinks, otherwise.

You Have to Pass

- Your RHO bid 1 ♠.

- You have a great heart suit, but now you can't bid 2 ♥ because it would make your partner think you are stronger than you are.

- 2 ♥ is not a jump bid in this example, like the 2 ♠ was in the previous example with nearly the identical hand. You have to pass.

Your Partner Bids First

- If you were the dealer, you would open this hand 2 ♠.

- But your partner was the dealer, and she opened up with 1 ♣.

- Now, instead, you respond 1 ♠, which says *at least* 6 points and *at least* four spades. Both are true, and you hope to be able to show more on your next bid.

REFINING THE WEAK TWO
Good discipline when making the bid allows for better communication

While many bids are universally used by all levels of players, so much of bridge communication is partnership agreement. For instance, in the fifties and sixties, opening on the two level would imply a very strong hand. Now most players play it as weak. Even within a bidding system, players have variations. Some partnerships prefer a bid to mean one thing,

but other equally successful players are a little more flexible.

The weak two is a perfect example. Some players like this bid to be very disciplined. The player making the bid will have two of the top three honors. Others don't care as much about suit quality. They like to make the bid with any long suit.

Both Majors

- In this hand you do have six hearts and between 5 to 10 high card points, but you also have four spades.

- If you're in the first or second seat, be quiet. Wait to see if your partner opens a minor or a spade.

- If your partner has passed, however, bid 2 ♥.

Look Where You're Sitting

- In this hand you have 6 high card points and 6 cards in the heart suit, but the quality of both your suit and your points is poor.

- In the first or second seat, you should pass.

- In the third seat, go ahead and bid 2 ♥.

I recommend that novice players play a more disciplined weak two system, at least in the first or second seat. So, if you're the first bidder of your partnership (in other words, you're in the first or second seat), then you should have two of the top three honors. Also, if you're thinking about opening diamonds, I wouldn't have 3-card support in either of the majors. You don't want to miss out on a major fit just because you prematurely jumped in with the diamonds. If you're in the third or fourth seat, however, anything goes (assuming your partner hasn't bid anything).

Sometimes you may have more than 6 cards. If you have a weak hand with 7 or 8 cards in a suit, you want to be even more aggressive. With 7 you can open on the three level. With 8 cards you can open on the four level.

In these cases, you don't have to be quite so disciplined with having two of the top three honors, although you might be more cautious if you're vulnerable and the opponents are not.

Too Strong

- Be careful not to get distracted by the length of your suit and forget that your hand must also be weak.

- Don't open on the two level just because you have a 6-card suit.

- This hand should be opened 1 ♥, not 2 ♥.

Three Level Bid

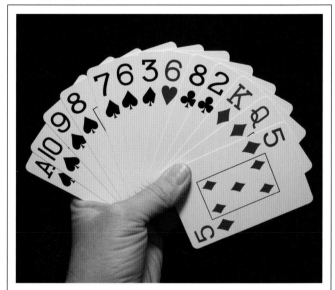

- In this hand, you have seven spades.

- This hand should be opened 3 ♠.

- It tells your partner that you have a 7-card spade suit and between 5 to 10 high card points.

WEAK PLUS WEAK

Your partner bids a weak two bid and you have a fit, but you are weak, too

The weak two bid is a bit of a gamble. Part of the motivation is the expectation that you have an outside chance to make your contract, but the other underlying motivation is that if you're weak, your opponents might have a bid somewhere. If you start on the two level, you make it harder for them to find their fit and communicate.

So if your partner opens with a weak two bid, you have to keep both these things in mind. You expect her to have a 6-card suit and between 5 to 10 high card points.

Look at the big picture. Your partner just announced to you that she's weak. You are also weak, so you can extrapolate and figure out that the opponents have all the points. And not

KNACK BRIDGE FOR EVERYONE

Continue the Preempt

- Your partner has opened 2 ♠, and your right hand opponent (RHO) has passed.

- Since you're weak and your partner is weak and your RHO passed, you can guess that the fourth bidder has a big hand.

- Continue the preempt by saying 3 ♠ to make it hard for her to bid.

A Big Gamble

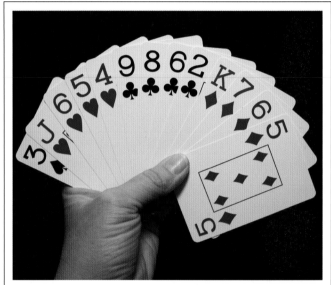

- Your partner has opened 2 ♦.

- Your RHO doubled.

- If you're not vulnerable, you should bid 5 ♦.

- You are so weak, they probably have game, but now they have to bid at the five level, which they might not make.

only are they likely to find a bid, it's likely to be a game bid.

This is a case where you want to continue the preempt. You do this assuming that the opponents will either leave you there, because they don't know what to bid, or they'll find it harder to get to their correct contract. Even if they leave you there and set you, the score will be less than what they would have gotten for getting game.

So now you have to look at the vulnerability to figure out how aggressive you should be. If the opponents are NOT vulnerable, they will get 420 for a game in a major. If they are

vulnerable, they will get 620 points. If you are not vulnerable, the opponents will get 50 points a trick for every trick they set you. If you are vulnerable, then they'll get 100 points a trick. If they double you, then the numbers will go up quickly.

So if you're vulnerable and they're not, perhaps just keep quiet. If you're both the same vulnerability, then raise your partner one level. If, however, they are vulnerable and you're not, then think about going all the way to the four or even five level to make it impossible for them to bid their game.

Vulnerable

- In this hand your partner has bid 2 ♠, and the opponent has bid 3 ♥.

- Since you are vulnerable, the penalty points will add up quickly if you're doubled.

- Even though you're weak and they probably have game, just bid 3 ♠ to make it harder for them to find the right contract.

Play Defense

- Your partner bid 2 ♥, and the opponent doubled.

- You have two hearts to support, so you have a fit, but you also have a nice spade holding—which is the suit they're most likely to choose.

- Stay quiet and hope they end up in spades.

- Or, if they choose a minor, they might get up too high.

AVERAGE & STRONG
What to do when you have a pretty good hand opposite your partner's weak bid

If your partner has bid a weak two bid, and you have an average hand—or even as many as 13 or 14 points—the philosophy of using the bid to interfere with the opponents goes away. They might not even be able to bid.

You also hope that your partner can actually make the 8 tricks he's gambled on. You have a little help for him, so leave

him there and you might get a plus score. If the opponents compete and bid a suit of their own, look at your points and shape and decide whether or not you have a better defensive or offensive hand.

If you are short in their suit, maybe you want to bid to steal the bid back. If you have a lot of the opponent's trump, then

Keep Quiet

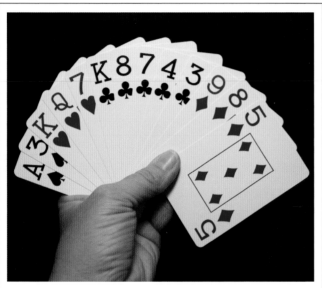

- Your partner has opened 2 ♠, and the opponent to your right has passed.

- Because you have 12 points, there's a good chance that neither opponent is strong enough to jump in at the two level.

- Just stay quiet and be confident you can make the 2 ♠ bid.

Raise Partner

- Your partner has opened 2 ♠ and the next player bids 3 ♥.

- Even though this hand is slightly weaker than the previous example, you need to jump in the bidding.

- Raise your partner to 3 ♠.

- He will know you're competing and that it's not an invitation to game.

maybe you're better off playing defense.

A strong hand gives you different options. If you have 15 points or more (or even a good 14), then you have a real chance for making a game—or possibly even slam. It depends on what's in both your hand and your partner's hand.

If you have a fit, you should go straight to 4 of that suit (assuming it's a major). You might not have the exact 16 points for game, but the shape of your partner's hand should help. If your partner has bid diamonds, and you have a fit with her, think about getting to no trump for the game if you have the other suits stopped. You should also think about no trump when you don't have a fit. And with a very strong hand, you can look for slam.

Bid Game

- Your partner opens 2 ♥.

- You have heart support and 15 points. Although there's a good chance that your partner has as few as 5 points, this is worth a game try.

- Bid 4 ♥ and cross your fingers.

Think about Slam

- Your partner has opened 2 ♥.

- Not only do you have great heart support, but you have a lot of points.

- You should be thinking about bidding slam. See the chapter on slam bidding to figure out how to do this.

POINTS, BUT NO FIT
Make an effort to get to no trump when you don't have a fit

As we discussed, if your partner makes a weak two bid and you have at least 15 points (or a good 14) in your hand, you should consider going to game. But what if you only have 1 card in your partner's suit? In that case, you want to see if you can get to 3NT.

First, let's talk about what we know about her hand. Your partner is in the first or second seat, so you can count on

her having two of the top three honors in her 6-card suit. (If you were in the first or second seat, you would have opened with your beautiful strong hand and the bidding would be completely different.) You also know that she has between 5 and 10 high card points.

A long suit can be just as valuable in no trump as it can in a trump suit, because no one can trump in and you can run

Mentioning a Feature

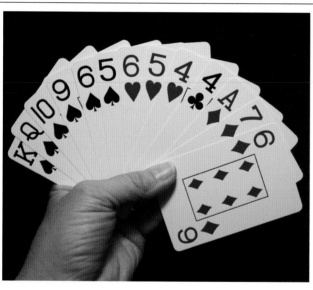

- You open 2 ♠, and your partner says 2NT.

- Your response here is 3 ♦.

- You are not saying that you have diamonds. You are saying, "Yes, I have a feature in diamonds that will help you get back to the dummy."

The Rebid

- This is your partner's hand.

- Now that you've told her that you have a feature

- in diamonds, she can feel comfortable in no trump.

- Her bid is 3NT.

the long suit. So now you need to find out if you can get to her long suit. There are a couple of different ways to do this, but the simplest method is something called "asking for a feature."

If your partner opens with a weak two, you bid 2NT. This is a demand bid that asks, "Partner, do you have another way for me to get to your hand besides your long suit?" If she does—usually an ace or protected king—she bids that suit. If she doesn't have an outside feature, she rebids her initial suit.

No Feature

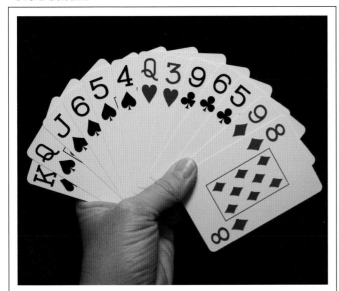

- You open 2 ♠, and your partner says 2NT.

- Your response here is 3 ♠.

- You have no way for your partner to get over to your spades after the ace of spades is knocked out.

  - Your hand is useless in no trump.

The Rebid

- This is your partner's hand.

- Realizing that she can't rely on tricks from you in no trump, she gambles that you can make game in

spades, even though you don't have a fit.

- Her bid is 4 ♠. With a weaker hand, she'd pass 3 ♠.

A DIFFERENT SUIT
When to change suits after your partner has preempted

While getting to no trump is an appealing prospect, players don't always have the right hand for that, even if they have a lot of points. If you open with a weak two bid and your partner chooses not to raise your suit or bid no trump, there's usually a good reason.

He might have a void, or a maybe a 6-card suit of his own. If you opened with a weak two bid, but your suit is diamonds,

maybe your partner has a diamond fit but a 6-card major. You'd rather be in his suit if you can. Or maybe he has a void in your suit, so he's reluctant to go to no trump, because then your hand is worthless.

In these cases, you have to have an agreement with your partner as to whether or not a change of suits is a forcing bid. Most players like it to be forcing for one round. If you have

Changing Suits

- Your partner has opened 2 ♦.

- You have a diamond fit, but you'd rather see if you can be in hearts.

- Your bid is 2 ♥.

- You can return to the diamonds if the hearts don't match up.

Stick with Partner's Suit

- You opened your hand and fell in love with it. Perhaps slam?

- But then your partner bids 4 ♠, implying eight spades and weak.

- It's tempting to try to take him out of spades, but you should leave him there.

- Your bid is pass.

3-card support or perhaps 2-card support with an honor, you should support your partner's suit.

This really applies to weak two bids. If, on the other hand, you're the partner of a player who just opened on the three or four level, you should remember two things. The first is that you only need 1 (or 0) cards in that suit to make a fit. And the second is that their hand is even more worthless outside of that trump suit. In this case, you might not want to change the suit even if you have a nice suit yourself. So, if you have a better than opening hand, raise their suit. Otherwise pass.

Void in Partner's Suit

- Your partner has opened with a bid of 2 ♥.

- You don't have a ton of points, but you also have no hearts.

- Bid your spade suit.

Rebid

- You opened 2 ♥.

- Then your partner bids 2 ♠, and you owe her a bid.

- Bid 3 ♦ to show your second suit.

- If you don't have a second suit, either raise her suit or rebid your suit.

20 OR 21 POINTS

If you have a balanced hand with these points, you should start at 2 no trump

Opening on the two level with spades, hearts, or diamonds shows a weak hand. Opening on the two level with no trump or clubs shows a strong hand—and a very specific amount of points. Just as 1NT limits the hand to exactly 15 to 17 points, 2NT is defined as exactly 20 or 21 points. (Turn the page to find out what you do with 18 or 19 points.)

The hand also needs to look like a no trump bid. In other words, it should be balanced. However, because the 2NT bid is used with so many points, players tend to be slightly less disciplined at this level. It's important to get the high point count message to your partner. Opening 2NT with a 5-card major is common and bidding it with two doubletons is not a problem.

Two No Trump

- This hand is a classic 2NT hand.

- You have no trump shape and 20 points.

- This is a passable bid.

Responding to 2 No Trump

- Assume your partner has bid 2NT, and this is your hand.

- You can treat it like a 1NT bid and bid Stayman to see if she has a 4-card major.

- Bid 3 ♣. If she answers 3 ♥, go to 4 ♥.

- If she answers 3 ♠, go to 3NT.

Treat the 2NT opener just as you would a 1NT opener. If you play Stayman and transfer over 1NT, then you should play them over 2NT. The only difference is the point count. You only need 5 points to do Stayman, because your partner has at least 20.

If you transfer, you can have 0 points—although you need to make sure you pass after the transfer if that's what your hand looks like.

If you don't have a hand that suits a transfer or Stayman bid, then you should bid 3NT with 5 to 10 points and look

for slam with more. As a matter of fact, if you have more than 10 points after a 2NT bid, you should be thinking of slam no matter what your hand looks like.

A 5-Card Suit

- Again, your partner has bid 2NT.

- You have a 5-card spade suit, so you should bid 3 ♥ to transfer to spades.

- After your partner says 3 ♠, you go to 3NT and let her pick which contract.

- If you don't play transfers, you can bid 3 ♠.

Staying in No Trump

- Your partner has bid 2NT.

- You don't have a 5- or 4-card major, so neither transfers nor Stayman is an option.

- In this case, it's all about points. Because you have 7 points and your partner has 20 or 21, you know you have enough for game.

- Bid 3NT and forget about your club suit.

18 OR 19 POINTS
How to show your points when you have that in-between number

The 18- or 19-point hand is the tricky hand. You have too many points for 1NT and too few for 2NT. What do you do?

The answer comes in the form of something called a jump shift. You begin by bidding 1 of a suit. Your next bid needs to jump a level and shift to another suit (or no trump).

The big fear with an 18- or 19-point hand is that the opponents and your partner are all going to follow with passes

and you'll be left in your puny 1 bid. But if your partner has fewer than 6 points, then you probably weren't going to be in game anyway. Be thankful that she didn't bid, and go ahead and make your easy one level contract.

However, most of the time, your partner will have at least 6 points and will make a bid. Now is the moment that you have to show her your points, because even though she's likely to

First Bid

- You'd love to open this hand 1NT. It's perfectly balanced and has no 4- or 5-card major.

- But you have one jack too many.

- Open this hand 1 ♣, knowing you'll be at no trump on the next bid.

Rebid

- This is your partner's hand. She responds to your 1 ♣ bid with a bid of 1 ♠.

- Now you jump to 2NT.

- This tells your partner that you have 18 or 19 points and a balanced hand.

- Looking at this hand and adding up the points, she can easily see that 3NT is the place to be.

have the 6 points, she is highly unlikely to have a bid beyond the one level.

Once you jump a level and shift suits, however, you have told her that you have 18 to 19 (sometimes 20) points, and now she can feel comfortable bidding again. You both know that you have game or close to game in points.

First Bid

- This hand exchanged one small club for a small spade, but you still open 1 ♣.

- With this hand, your rebid is going to depend on what your partner bids.

- They should all be a jump or jump shift.

Possible Rebids for This Hand
If partner bids . . .

- I diamond, bid 2 spades.

- I heart, bid 2 spades.

- I spade, bid 4 spades.

- 1NT, bid 2NT.

135

22 OR MORE POINTS
Getting a hand that's as big as it gets

If you have a 20- or 21-point hand and you bid 2NT, you're generally not going to get passed by your partner. She knows just how big your hand is, so unless she has fewer than 5 points, she'll probably try to eke out a bid. If she does pass you, then you're actually quite happy not being any higher, since you know she has a bust hand.

However, let's say you have 24 points. Bidding 2NT under-values your hand, and you might not have the right shape for it anyway. But you can't bid on the one level, because it would be a tragedy if your partner passes your bid. You can't bid on the two or three level, because it implies a long suit with a weak hand. You can't bid on the four level, as you don't know anything about her hand yet. You need some way to make your partner bid. Your forcing bid is 2 ♣.

Typical 2 ♣ Hand

- This hand has 23 points. Your bid is 2 ♣.

- It says nothing about your clubs. It just shows 22 or more points and is a forcing bid.

- After your partner bids, you will bid your heart suit.

Atypical 2 ♣ Bid

- With this hand, you only have 16 points.

- Nonetheless, you are going to lose no spade tricks (you can trump them), no heart tricks, 1 diamond trick, and 1 club trick. So this hand makes 5 ♥ without any help from your partner.

- Bid 2 ♣ to find out something from your partner.

- You might get to slam.

Remember, bidding 2 ♠, 2 ♥, or 2 ♦ implies a weak hand, but I mentioned that you couldn't use it for clubs. The reason is that we need to preserve that club bid to show a big hand—22 or more points—by the opener. It's the only forcing bid by the opener.

The 2 ♣ bid says nothing about any suit. It only talks about points. When you bid it, your partner can count on you to have 22 or more points. However, as always, there are exceptions to the rule. You might not have 22+ points but would still bid 2 ♣ precisely because it is a forcing bid (Example 2).

No Trump Hand

- This hand is perfectly balanced and begging to be in no trump.

- The old way of bidding would have you say 3NT right off the bat here, but most people now would bid 2 ♣ with this hand.

- With the 2 ♣ bid, you find out more about your partner's hand.

This hand has only 16 high card points, but if you find your partner with either the ace of diamonds or the ace of clubs, you make a small slam.

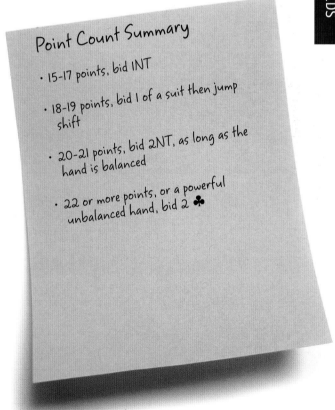

Point Count Summary

- 15-17 points, bid 1NT

- 18-19 points, bid 1 of a suit then jump shift

- 20-21 points, bid 2NT, as long as the hand is balanced

- 22 or more points, or a powerful unbalanced hand, bid 2 ♣

137

STEP RESPONSE
One method of responding to a 2 ♣ bid

The step response to a 2 ♣ bid is probably the least popular system among experts, but it's one that can be very helpful to a novice player. It's the simplest to learn, and it gives very specific information right away.

The step response system is *forcing for two rounds*. After your partner bids 2 ♣, you begin by communicating the point value of your hand:

0 - 3 points	2 ♦
4 - 6 points	2 ♥
7 - 9 points	2 ♠
10+ points	2 NT

After you make your "point count" bid, your partner (the 2 ♣ opener) will come back with either her 5-card suit or 2NT

Response to 2 ♣

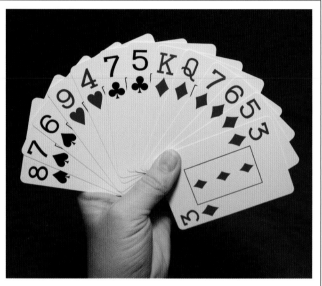

- With this hand, you would respond 2 ♥ using step response.

- This shows 4 to 6 points. It says nothing about your hearts.

- If your partner now bids spades, you bid 3 ♠.

- If she bids anything else, you bid diamonds to show your suit.

Response to 2 ♣

- With this hand, you would respond 2 ♠.

- This shows 7 to 9 points. It says nothing about your spades.

- Whatever your partner bids, you will be able to support.

if she's balanced. If she's bid her 5-card (or longer) suit, you must bid again at this point. Do not pass, even if you have 0 points in your hand. Remember your partner has *at least* 22 points. She may have more. She may have enough for game all by herself, but she just wants to find out more about your suit.

Here are your options:

1. If you like her 5-card suit, repeat it.
2. If you don't like her 5-card suit,
    a. mention your suit.
    b. go to no trump if you are balanced.

If she bids 2NT, it's a little different. First of all, you can start treating it just like she'd opened a no trump to begin with. In other words, use transfers if you have a 5-card major or use Stayman if you have at least one 4-card major.

The only time that a 2 ♣ bid is only forcing for one round is when you've bid 2 ♦ in response and your partner goes to 2NT. If you have no points and no suit, then you can leave her there.

Response to 2 ♣

- With this hand, you would respond 2 ♦.

- This shows 0 to 3 points.

- Because you have the 3 points, not less, you should bid again no matter what your partner bids.

Response to 2 ♣

- With this hand, you would also respond 2 ♦, again showing 0 to 3 points.

- Because you have only 1 point, you should bid if your partner bids a suit. Pass if she bids 2NT.

- If the opener has 25 or more points, she'll jump to 3NT.

139

WAITING RESPONSE

Originally this was the natural response, but now it is often called two diamonds waiting

The natural response system, a.k.a. the two diamonds waiting response, is the most widely used response system, but even within this system there are variations, so if you're going to use this system with a partner, make sure you're both on the same page.

Traditionally, with this system, the opener bids 2 ♣ and the responder bids 2 ♦ with a weak hand: 6 or fewer points. Game is possible—depending on the 2 ♣ bidder's hand—but not necessarily a guarantee.

If the responder bids anything else (2 ♥, 2 ♠, 2NT, 3 ♣, or 3 ♦), he has a stronger hand and the suit or shape he has mentioned. Game is a definite and slam is a possibility.

Two ♦

- Your partner has bid 2 ♣.

- With this hand you bid 2 ♦.

- It says nothing about your diamonds, but it does limit your hand to 8 points or fewer.

- Your partner will bid his best suit. It's a forcing bid.

Another Two ♦

- With this hand you also bid 2 ♦ over the 2 ♣ bid, even though it looks much more interesting.

- If your partner bids spades, you support him.

- If he bids no trump, transfer to hearts.

- If he bids a minor, bid the hearts.

Alternatively, some players like to reverse the bid. The 2 ♦ response shows a hand with points that is waiting to hear more about the opponent's suit or shape. Any other bid shows a bust hand with length in that particular suit.

And finally, there's a hybrid of the two. Two ♦ is positive and waiting. Three ♣ shows a bust hand without points and without a suit (some players play that 2 ♥ shows a bust hand). If you bid anything but 2 ♦ or 3 ♣, it means you have 9 or more points and at least five cards in the suit you bid. You're interested in slam.

The hybrid tends to be the most popular form of the two diamond waiting bid used today, so that is what I will use in the examples on this page.

Slam Interest

- Here's the same hand with a few more points.

- In this case, you bid 2 ♥.

- You are describing a nice heart suit and at least 9 points.

- You're interested in slam.

Bust Hand

- In this hand, you have 1 point and you have no long suit.

- After your partner bids 2 ♣, you should bid 3 ♣.

- Your partner will now place the contract knowing that you have no points and no long suit.

141

CONTROLS

A refinement to the point count, a.k.a. step response, system

This system is something that counts "controls," and controls can be defined as aces and kings. With aces and kings, you can control the suit—at least for a round or two. If you're looking to bid slam, they are key cards to have.

This is a very similar system to the step response, except that (for the most part) it eliminates the queens and the jacks. While queens and jacks do have their worth, they are slightly overvalued by the 4-3-2-1 point system. If you're playing steps you might find yourself up in the slam area without some pretty important cards.

An ace is obviously most valuable, so an ace counts as two controls. A king is one control. This is only used after your partner bids 2 ♣, and here are the responses:

2 ♦ : 0 or 1 control

Two ♦

- In this hand you have just the king of hearts.

- Your bid in response to 2 ♣ would be 2 ♦ using controls.

- This shows zero or 1 control.

- You would make this same bid with no king as well.

More Points

- In this hand, you also bid 2 ♦ over a 2 ♣ bid, showing that you have 0 or 1 control.

- This time you actually have 6 points, but because they are in queens and jacks, you don't count them.

- This is where controls really differs from step response.

2 ♥: 2 controls
2 ♠: 3 controls

This can also be translated to say:
2 ♦: a king or less
2 ♥: an ace or two kings
2 ♠: an ace and a king, or three kings

Or if you translate it to point count:
2 ♦: 0–3

2 ♥: 4–6
2 ♠: 7–9

And that looks pretty darn similar to step response without the queens and jacks. The only difference is that 2 aces would be only 8 points in steps, putting it squarely in the "spade" response, but it would be four controls, which puts it at 2NT, with the control response system.

Two ♥

- In this hand you have the king of hearts and the king of clubs.

- Your bid in response to 2 ♣ would be 2 ♥.

- This shows two controls.

Two ♠

- In this hand you have an ace and a king.

- Your bid in response to 2 ♣ would be 2 ♠.

- This shows three controls.

143

RECOGNIZING A SLAM

A couple of strong hands opposite each other can mean a potential slam bid

Generally speaking, it's thought that if you have 33 points between you and your partner, you can probably make a small slam. And if you have 37 points between you and your partner, then you have a good shot at a grand slam. When you remember that there are only 40 points in the deck, you realize that this isn't much of a surprise. You also realize that

this probably doesn't happen very often.

Nonetheless, because the payoff is so big—both in terms of points and the tremendous satisfaction you get for bidding and making a slam—bridge players have developed some systems to help them figure out whether or not they should be in slam, and many of them are described in this chapter.

Don't Close Out

- Your partner has bid 1 ♠.

- You know that you not only have a spade fit, but you have a huge amount of points as well.

- You have to make sure you make a forcing bid.

- Change suits or start your ace asking right away. More on how to do this later.

After 2 ♣

- Your partner has bid 2 ♣.

- No matter which 2 ♣ response system you use, your response will tell her that you're interested in slam.

- You don't have to worry about either of you stopping before you get to slam.

When you realize that you and your partner have the points to go to slam, you have to be careful not to close out the suit if your partner is not entirely aware of your points.

Also, you should keep in mind that the 33- and 37-point count suggestions are just that. They are guidelines for you to use, but many hands can make a slam with far fewer points. Sometimes it's the shape that matters much more than the total point count. And sometimes you can have the points and the slam will still fail.

I find that novices tend to avoid bidding slam no matter what.

In some sense, this isn't a bad strategy at this level. A safe game bid is a bird in the hand after all. And frequently the slam falls through on a bad trump split or a finesse that doesn't work. On the flip side, you're going to have to get there sometime if you want to be competitive in duplicate bridge.

Unusual Shape

- In this hand, you're the opener and you're interested in slam, even though you don't have a ton of points.

- If you play controls, you may want to bid 2 ♣ with this hand. It would be helpful with a step response system as well.

  - If you don't, you should jump to ace asking after your first bid.

After 1 No Trump

- Your partner has bid 1NT.

- You have 18 points, so even at her lowest range, you know that you have the 33 points needed for a small slam.

- You're not worried about the clubs, because your partner's points have to be somewhere!

145

BLACKWOOD
A convention to ask for aces

Blackwood is a simple ace-asking convention. You and your partner have generally agreed on a suit (sometimes no trump), and now you think you may have slam, but you'd like to know if you have all the top cards before you go wildly taking the bidding up to the six level.

It's time to use Blackwood. Your bid is 4NT. Because 4NT is beyond the game level, it's unusual enough that (a) it's not used very often for anything natural and (b) it's going to catch your partner's eye. She'll know it's a specific request for her to respond with the number of aces she has. Here are her responses:

5 ♣: 0 or 4 aces   5 ♥: 2 aces
5 ♦: 1 ace   5 ♠: 3 aces

Answering with Aces

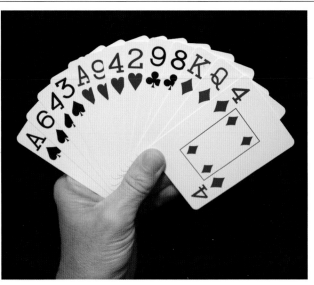

- After you agreed on hearts as the trump suit, your partner bid 4NT.

- You have two aces, so your bid is 5 ♥.

- If that's all your partner needed, she'll ask for kings.

- If she's still missing an ace, she'll leave it at 5 ♥.

Choosing to Ask

- Your partner opened 1NT, and you have 16 points as well. But you have a few holes.

- Transfer to spades. After your partner bids spades, jump to 4NT to ask for aces.

- If she comes back with three, you'll know you're in good shape for slam.

Simple, right? And it really is just that simple. Once your partner bids, you'll have an accurate account of the four aces. If you don't have all four aces, you can be pretty confident you're going to lose at least one trick. If there's any chance you'll be losing another trick, then you should probably sign off at five and forget about slam. If, however, you do have all four aces, then you should look for kings.

The bidding is the same, just up one level. Bidding 5NT asks for kings, and here are the familiar responses:

5 ♣: 0 or 4 kings
5 ♦: 1 king
5 ♥: 2 kings
5 ♠: 3 kings

Once you get the answer, then you place the contract.

Another Try

- You begin by bidding 2 ♣ and eventually find your spade fit.

- You know you have 4 ♠ cold, but your hand is looking pretty good for slam.

- Bid 4NT to see if your partner has either or both of the minor suit aces.

- If you played controls, you'd already know.

No Point

- Sometimes there's no point in asking because you know the answer.

- If you bid 2 ♣ with this hand and your partner answered 2 ♦ with either steps or controls, you know that she can't have those two missing aces.

- Even though it looks amazing, slam still isn't there.

147

OVER NO TRUMP

Use Gerber or quantitative bidding to find slam after your partner bids no trump

When the bid has started or ended in a natural no trump bid, then you have a couple of other options. You can use the Gerber ace-asking method. Gerber is very similar to Blackwood, but it starts lower, which can be a real help if you find you're missing too many pieces.

The bid to ask for aces using Gerber is 4 ♣. Most players use this only after no trump bids, because it's too easy to confuse a 4 ♣ bid for a natural club bid.

Just as in Blackwood, the responder goes up the ladder counting aces:

4 ♦: 0 or 4 aces	4 ♠: 2 aces
4 ♥: 1 ace	4NT: 3 aces

Gerber

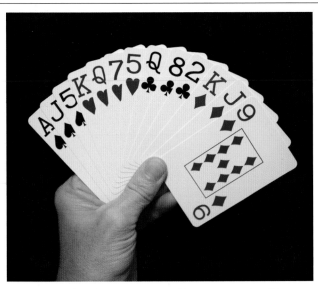

- You opened 1NT. Your partner immediately jumped to 4 ♣.

- You should take this for Gerber, asking for aces.

- Your response is 4 ♥, meaning one ace.

Partner's Hand

- This is the hand that bid Gerber.

- With your bid of 4 ♥, you've shown one ace. That's not enough.

- You're really unlikely to make slam in no trump, missing two aces.

- She signs off at 4NT.

As you can see, this keeps the bidding much lower, and a pair can sign off in 4NT if they choose.

Another way to bid over no trump is to bid quantitatively. When you make a 1NT bid, you're saying that you have 15 to 17 points. It doesn't seem like a big range, but those 3 points could make a difference.

If your partner bids 4NT over your 1NT, she's not asking for aces (remember, she could have used Gerber if that's what she's interested in). She's asking you to bid 6NT if you have 17 and to pass if you have 15. If she bids 5NT, she's asking you to bid 6NT with 15 and 7NT with 17 points. With 16 you have to look at your values. Are your points aces and kings? Are they well placed?

The quantitative hands are used when a player has 16 or 17 points opposite an opening no trump bid. Because you should really have 33 points to bid slam, a 15-point hand just isn't quite enough, but you don't want to miss it if it's a 17-point hand.

Quantitative

- Another way to look for slam over no trump is to make a quantitative bid.

- You bid 1NT with this hand.

- Your partner says 4NT.

- You pass, because you're at the low end of your points.

A Good 16

- You bid 1NT, and your partner said 4NT.

- You don't have the maximum, but you do have a really solid 5-card diamond suit.

- This one is worth the gamble.

- Bid 6NT.

ROMAN KEY CARD

A more refined system that lets you find out about the king and queen of trump

Some slam hands sound absolutely great in the bidding until the hand comes down and you realize you're at 6 ♠ without either the king or the queen of spades. That could easily happen if you're bidding and discover that you have all the aces and three of the kings. In any other suit, you're fine, but the suit you've chosen as trump is the one where you're missing the king. And because we don't ask about queens, you find you're missing that too.

The Roman Key Card system (also called Roman Key Card Blackwood or RKC) was developed to correct for this problem. It recognizes that the king of trump is as important as the aces and that the queen of trump is pretty important, too.

Showing Key Cards

- After you've agreed on spades, your partner has said 4NT.

- Now you count your aces and the king of trump.

- You do not have the king of spades, and you only have one ace.

- With this hand, you respond 5 ♣. You have 1 key card.

Three Key Cards

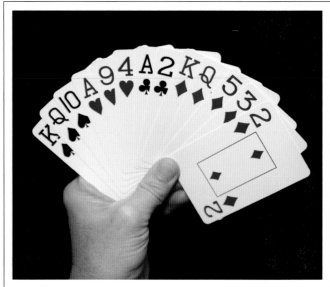

- Assuming spades are still trump, you can see that you have 3 key cards.

- You have two aces and the king of trump.

- You should bid 5 ♦.

- You also have the queen of trump, but you can't indicate that yet.

The asking part of RKC is the same. The asker bids 4NT. The responses are how this system differs. To begin with, you aren't just counting the four aces. In this, there are 5 key cards: the four aces, plus the king of trump. This system is called RKC 1430:

- 5 ♣: 1 or 4 key cards
- 5 ♦: 3 or 0 key cards
- 5 ♥: 2 but no queen of trump
- 5 ♠: 2 with the queen of trump

Some players reverse the two minor suit bids and play what's referred to as 3014:

- 5 ♣: 3 or 0 key cards
- 5 ♦: 1 or 4 key cards
- 5 ♥: 2 but no queen of trump
- 5 ♠: 2 with the queen of trump

You'll find expert players on both sides, and it doesn't really matter as long as you and your partner are on the same page.

The Queen

- After you've agreed on spades, your partner has said 4NT.

- You have 2 key cards here, so your bid will be either hearts or spades.

- Now you check to see if you also have the queen of hearts.

- You do, so your bid is 5 ♠.

Two, No Queen

- This is the exact same situation as last time.

- After you've agreed on spades, your partner has said 4NT.

- You have 2 key cards here, so your bid will be either hearts or spades.

- This time you do not have the queen of spades, so you bid 5 ♥.

MORE ROMAN KEY CARD
Taking RKC a step further

If you thought that was all there was to Roman Key Card, guess again. The next step in Roman Key Card involves the kings and the queen of trump.

If you know you have the queen, then you're only concerned about the side suit kings. Bid 5NT here. This is like regular Blackwood 5NT, although it only asks about side suit kings—not the king of trump, because that's already been

part of your count:

6 ♣: 0 side suit kings
6 ♦: 1 side suit king
6 ♥: 2 side suit kings
6 ♠: 3 side suit kings

Asking for Kings

- Spades are trump, and your partner bid 4NT.

- You answered 5 ♥, showing 2 key cards, with no queen of trump.

- Now your partner has bid 5NT.

- You answer 6 ♦, showing one king. You don't count your king of spades since you've already provided that information.

Asking for the Queen

- Again, spades are trump, and after your partner bid 4NT, you bid 5 ♣, showing your 1 key card.

- Now your partner bids 5 ♦. She is wondering if you have the queen of trump.

- You do, so you answer with your side suit king. You say 6 ♦.

If, however, you're looking for the trump queen, then the bidding gets a bit more complicated. You can't ask for side suit kings, though with the bidding you'll still find out about them.

Your bid to ask for the queen is the next cheapest bid that is NOT trump. For example, if your partner said 5 ♣, then you know he has 1 or 4 key cards. Your bid of 5 ♦ asks about the queen of trump. Don't worry about getting up too high, because if you want to know about the queen, then obviously

your partner has bid either 5 ♣ or 5 ♦. A higher bid would already have told you about the queen.

Now it gets even trickier. If you don't have the queen of trump, then you bid the trump suit at the cheapest level. If you do have the queen, you now bid a suit with a side suit king, as long as it isn't higher than 6 of the trump suit. If your side suit king is higher, then bid 5NT to show the queen, plus the side suit king.

Another Example

- This time hearts are trump, and you're the ace asker.

- Your partner has answered with 5 ♦, meaning 3 or 0 key cards.

- You now want to ask about the queen. You say 5 ♠, because 5 ♥ would be a sign off.

Responding

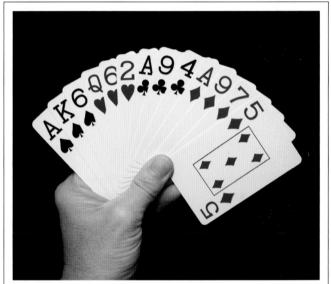

- This is the hand that's responding to the 5 ♠ bid asking for the queen.

- You have the queen, but your only side suit king is the king of spades. If you say 6 ♠, you'll be up too high.

- Respond with 5NT. This implies a side suit king in a suit higher than trump. It therefore must be spades.

153

CUE BIDDING ACES
Another way to figure out if you have slam possibilities

Blackwood, whether RKC or not, is great, but there are times when you need to know about specific aces, not just the number of aces. You might have 33 points between the two of you, but if the 7 points you're missing are the ace and king of the same suit, then it doesn't really matter.

Also, it's not terribly helpful when you have a void. You find out the number of aces your partner has, but what if between the two of you, you're missing an ace. Is it the one in your void or is it the one you need? You may find that the two of you are overvaluing your partner's hand when hers doesn't match up with yours. Because of these shortcomings, some players like to use a series of cue bids to figure out specific aces and voids. Once they decide on a suit, they cue bid suits, up the line, to show first round control.

Missing Ace

- You opened 1 ♠. Your partner jumped to 3 ♠, so now you're looking for slam.

- You need to know if you can stop the diamonds.

- If you can't, you don't want to be in 5 ♠, so ace asking would be a disaster here, and a cue bid would be perfect.

- Bid 4 ♣, showing first round control in clubs.

Partner's Hand

- This is the partner of the previous example.

- After the cue bid of 4 ♣, she would bid 4 ♦, showing the ace of diamonds.

- Now the opener can comfortably go to 6 ♠.

154

For instance, if your partner has just bid 4 ♠, but you're interested in going on, you could bid 4NT or you could cue bid. If you bid 5 ♣, you're showing first round control in clubs. This would mean an ace or a void in clubs.

Your partner would then respond in diamonds if he could. If not, then he'd respond in hearts, and if he couldn't do that either, then he'd just go right back to 5 ♠.

Another Example

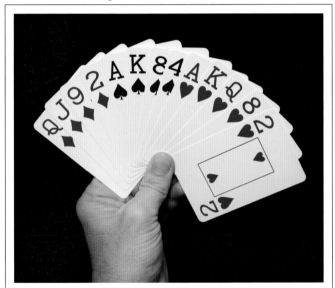

- You opened 1 ♥ and your partner jumped to 3 ♥.

- Ace asking won't help, because you really need to know specifically about the diamonds.

- If she came back with one ace, you'd be stuck as to what to do next.

- Bid 3 ♠, cue bidding your spade ace.

The Other Hand

- This is the partner of the previous hand.

- She's bid her 3 ♠ cue bid, showing her ace of spades. You bid 4 ♣, showing the club ace.

- Now, she'll sign off in 4 ♥. Clearly it was the diamond ace she needed.

- You can now show her that ace, bidding 5 ♦.

OVERCALL PHILOSOPHY
When your right hand opponent bids, you become the overcaller

In previous chapters, I think I've made it clear that you need 13 points to open your hand for your partnership. When your partner hears your bid, she's going to count on you for at least that amount and evaluate her hand and your chances accordingly. However, once the opponents have started the bidding, your strategy necessarily has to change.

If you stick rigidly to the "must have 13 points to open for

my partnership," you'll make it much easier for your opponents to end up in the right contract. If, instead, you interfere, they might either end up in the wrong suit or be up too high in their efforts to compete.

So if you're the person directly following the opener, be a little more aggressive. This person is called the overcaller, and the general rule of thumb is that you should have at least 10

Good Suit

- Let's say your right hand opponent (RHO) bid 1 ♠.

- You only have 11 points, but you have a nice heart suit. Go ahead bid 2 ♥.

- Not only does it tell your partner what suit to lead, but it also takes up a lot of bidding space.

No Suit

- Your RHO bid 1 ♥.

- You have 13 points here, but no suit to bid.

- You have to pass.

- If your 2 of hearts was a 2 of spades, you could double.

points and least 5 cards in the suit you're bidding.

While it's frustrating sometimes when the opponents have opened and made your bid difficult, the upside is that you now have a chance to bid a weaker hand. You're no longer opening in a vacuum. The opponents have bid, and you're put in a defensive position. Should you try to steal the bid? Should you try to set them? Maybe you can interfere with the bidding sequence and make it hard for them to find their perfect fit.

If you have a nice suit, even if you don't have the points, then it's worth jumping in with a bid. The first picture below is a perfect example of a good overcall.

No Trump

- Notice that this hand is exactly like the other hand, with one significant difference—more points.

- You have 16 points, a balanced hand, and you can stop the heart suit twice.

- Now, when your RHO bids 1 ♥, you can easily say 1NT.

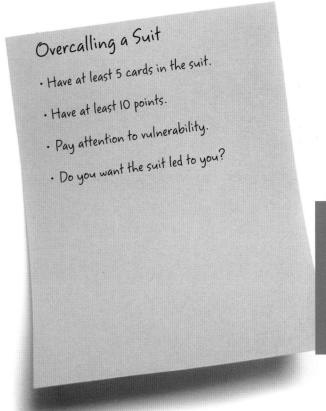

Overcalling a Suit

- Have at least 5 cards in the suit.

- Have at least 10 points.

- Pay attention to vulnerability.

- Do you want the suit led to you?

THE UPSIDE
Why it's good to make an overcall

When you get more familiar with the bidding process, you'll realize how much information you and your partner can convey to each other using only those 15 words. The process gets a whole lot harder, however, when the opponents jump into the conversation.

This is the main reason most bridge players like to drop the points for the overcall bid. If you had to have 13 points, there would be far fewer opportunities and your opponents would find it easier to communicate. Interfere and just maybe they'll end up in the wrong spot.

The other great reason to overcall is to tell your partner what to lead. If the opponents are bidding, chances are that they'll have the points to keep bidding despite your interference, which means you and your partner will be on defense.

Good Suit

- Your right hand opponent (RHO) bid 1 ♠.

- You have 11 points, but most of your points are concentrated in one suit. You would be fine if your partner led this suit.

- Bid 2 ♣.

- It also prevents the responder from bidding 1NT.

Good Points

- Your RHO bid 1 ♠.

- In this hand, your suit is lousy, but you have a real opener.

- In this case, overcall your heart suit, even though it's not strong. The points in your side suit make up for it.

Getting your partner off to the right lead could be critical toward finding the perfect defense to defeat a contract.

Sometimes you do get left in your bid, and if you've chosen the right hand and the right time to make your overcall, then you will almost always be successful. Even if are set a trick, the opponents will only get 50 points, versus 110 or 140, 170, or even 420, depending on what they bid and what they can make. Remember, ultimately it's not about bidding to the most successful contract; it's about getting the best possible score for the hand.

Take up Space

- Your RHO bid 1 ♦.

- In this case, your suit isn't fantastic, but it's not terrible, and you take up a ton of bidding space. Bid 2 ♣.

- Now, the responder can't bid a 4-card major.

Favorable Vulnerability

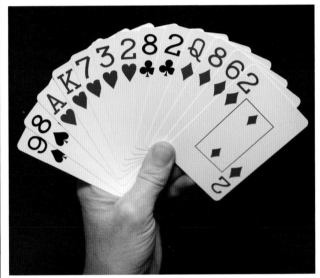

- The vulnerability is favorable when the opponents are vulnerable and you are not.

- The opponents will be cautious because their penalty is big. You can be more aggressive.

- Bid 1 ♥ after the dealer opens to show your partner what suit to compete in.

OVERCALLS

THE DOWNSIDE
Sometimes it's better to just keep quiet

While an overcall bid can be very satisfying when your interference prevents the opponents from finding the right suit or getting to game, it can also have some pitfalls.

First, remember that it's going to tell your partner what to lead. You may have the requisite 5-card suit and 10 points, but whatever you bid is also going to be what your partner leads. It doesn't get your defense off to the right start when your only honor card in the suit gets sucked up by the opponent's ace.

Even if you are comfortable bidding your suit as a lead director, you also have to realize that you've just given the opponents some information. They know what your best suit is, they know who is likely to have the missing honor cards—you had to have some points to bid after all!—and it might give

Bad Suit

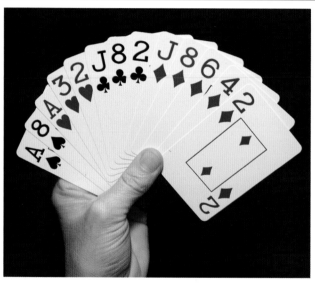

- Your opponent bid 1 ♣.

- You have 10 points and a 5-card diamond suit, but this is not a good overcall.

- Your bid barely interferes with their bidding, and it certainly doesn't get the defense off to a good lead.

Bad Shape

- Your right hand opponent (RHO) bid 1 ♣.

- Don't get tempted to bid 1 ♦ here. You do not have a 5-card suit.

- Yes, a diamond is a good lead, and yes, you have 13 points, but you still have to pass.

the responder an opportunity for a more descriptive bid.

Remember the negative double from Chapter 10? If the opponent has bid a minor and you bid a major, the responder can now be very specific about whether or not he has four or five in his major. Without the overcall, the bid of 1 of a major just promised 4 *or more*. It wasn't very specific.

Finally, you might find yourself in over your head if your opponents can't think of what to bid. Your partner might only have a few points and not much support. He keeps quiet, and you get stuck.

Too Weak	*Too Strong*

- Your RHO bid 1 ♥.

- Here's another tempting hand. You have a nice spade suit, and all your points are concentrated there, but you should still pass.

- Your partner is going to expect all of that *and* 10 points. You only have 7 points.

- Your RHO bid 1 ♣.

- This hand has a fabulous suit, and a huge amount of points, but you don't want to overcall 1 ♠.

- If you have 19 points, and your RHO has 13 points,

that only leaves 8 points, split between the other two players.

- They both might pass and you'd be stuck at 1 ♠.

- Double instead to at least force a bid.

BIG HAND OVERCALLS

The bid to make with more points and stoppers in the opponent's suit

Because an overcall could be as few as 10 points, you need to have some way to show your partner that you have a much bigger hand. If you have only 13 or 14 points, the simple overcall is fine. If you have 15 or more, however, then you need to think about doing something different.

If you have between 15 to 17 points, then you have no

trump values. Do you have no trump shape? And more importantly, are you able to stop the suit that the opponent bid? This is critical. You can be certain that the partner of the bidder will be leading that suit if you stay in no trump. You probably want to be able to stop it twice or to have length in that suit.

Good No Trump Overcall

- Your right hand opponent (RHO) bid 1 ♠.

- You have 17 points and the spades stopped twice. You really don't have a suit to bid.

- Bid 1NT because it describes your hand perfectly.

Bad No Trump Overcall

- Your RHO bids 1 ♠.

- Even though you have 16 points and a balanced hand, you can't stop the spades.

- You also have no aces, so if you win the auction, you're going to have to lose the lead to set up some of your suits.

- Bid 2 ♦ to show your 5-card suit.

No trump is such a descriptive and handy bid—primarily because both you and your partner have so many tools at your disposal to get to the right spot—that you should make every effort to bid it if you can. If you feel you can comfortably stop the opponent's suit, then you should go ahead and bid 1NT. If you can't, then you hope you have another bid: either a 5-card suit or perhaps a double if you're short in the opponent's suit.

The double is also the bid if you have more than the 15 to 17 points of no trump. It's one of the few forcing bids you can make in the overcall seat. If you have a lot of points, you absolutely do not want your partner to pass. Make the double bid, even if you have a great suit of your own. Your partner will initially view it as a takeout double and give you her best suit, but as soon as you bid a different suit, she should recognize that you doubled to show a big hand.

Double

- Your RHO bid 1 ♠.

- You have a balanced hand and 17 points. You would have opened this 1NT if you'd been the first bidder, but after the 1 ♠ bid, doubling is a better bid.

- You're short in spades and can support everything else.

- It's especially good that you have four of the other major, because that would be your partner's first choice bid.

Double

- Again, the RHO bid 1 ♠.

- This is a pretty powerful hand. You will almost certainly make 4 ♥.

- If you jump to 4 ♥ you might miss a slam.

- If you only bid 2 ♥, your partner might pass.

- Double and find something out about your partner's hand.

MICHAELS CUE BID

Sometimes being in the overcall seat gives you a way to describe your shape

Occasionally you'll get a hand that seems great, but really doesn't have the points to be an opening hand. If you have a 6- or 7-card suit, you can open on the two or three level to show your partner that you're weak but you have a great trump suit.

But what if you have two 5-card suits? You can't bid on the two level, because that implies a 6-card suit, but your two 5-card suits mean that you also have either a singleton and a doubleton or a void and a triple. This makes your hand much more interesting. Often shape can be just as valuable as, if not more valuable than, high card points.

If you're the opener, you can't bid this hand yet. But if you're in the overcall seat, you can jump in. However, since you're

Weak Michaels

- Your right hand opponent (RHO) bid 1 ♠.

- You cue bid 2 ♠. This shows five of the other major (hearts) and five of a minor.

- With 3-card support, your partner will bid hearts.

- You should pass the 3 ♥ bid. Your goal was to steal the bid, not try to get to game.

Asking about the Minor

- The bidding has been 1 ♠, 2 ♠ (your partner's Michaels cue bid), and then a pass.

- You don't have the hearts, so you want to ask what the minor suit is.

- Bid 2NT. Don't make the mistake of bidding your minor suit. Chances are, it's the other minor that works for your partner.

weak, you don't really have the points to take two bids. Because of that, a bridge player named Mike Michaels came up with a convention that has been widely adopted for this exact situation.

He suggested that you use the opener's bid to your advantage. You cue bid the opener's suit to show your two-suited hand. If the opener has bid a minor, you cue bid that same minor to show two 5-card majors. If the opener has bid a major, you cue bid that same major to show five of the other major and five of an unspecified minor suit.

With a minor cue bid, the partner of the cue bidder picks one of the majors, whichever one is better for him. With a major cue bid, the partner of the cue bidder looks to see if he has 3-card support for the other major. If he does, he bids that. If he does not, then he should now bid 2NT. This asks the cue bidder which minor he has.

The Michaels cue bid can be used with a weak hand or a strong hand. If you have regular opening points, you are better off doing a regular overcall. You can offer your second suit at a second bid.

Strong Michaels

- Your opponents bid 2 ♦, showing a weak hand with a 6-card suit.

- You have a lot of points and a two-suited hand.

- Cue bidding 3 ♦ forces your partner to bid and describes your hand perfectly—two 5-card majors.

- You should take it to game after your partner chooses the major.

Regular Overcall

- Your RHO bid 1 ♥.

- You have a two-suited hand, but because you have a regular opening hand, you should overcall your spade suit rather than bidding Michaels.

- You have a second bid with your diamond suit if your partner bids.

UNUSUAL NO TRUMP

Another two-suited convention you can use in conjunction with the Michaels cue bid

Before the Michaels cue bid was invented, there was a similar convention called the Unusual No Trump. This bid also shows two-suited hands. It is a jump to 2NT in the overcall seat.

Initially the Unusual No Trump was designed to show two 5-card or longer *minor* suits. Now most people play it in conjunction with Michaels to show the two lowest unbid suits,

although frequently that does still tend to be the minors.

For instance, if your opponent bids 1 ♠, you jump bid 2NT to show five clubs and five diamonds. If he bids 1 ♥, you jump to 2NT to show the same five clubs and five diamonds.

If, on the other hand, the opponent bids 1 ♣, then a jump to 2NT shows five diamonds and five hearts—the two lowest

Unusual No Trump

- Your right hand opponent (RHO) bid 1 ♥.

- You have two 5-card minors. After an opener in a major, bid 2NT. This shows the two lowest unbid suits using Unusual No Trump convention.

- It describes your hand perfectly and takes up a lot of the bidding options for the opponents.

Over a Minor

- Your RHO bid 1 ♣.

- Your bid here is again 2NT. It shows the two lowest unbid suits—hearts and diamonds.

- If the opponent had instead bid one ♠, you could have said 2 ♠ with this hand—a Michaels bid showing the other major and a minor.

unbid suits. If the opponent bids 1 ♦, then a jump to 2NT shows five clubs and five hearts—again, the two lowest unbid suits.

The partner now looks at his hand and decides which of the two suits is a better fit. He bids that suit on the three level. It seems a little risky to be bidding that high, but it's good for two reasons. As I mentioned before, because your hand is shapely, you actually have a lot more power than your points indicate. Also, you've taken up a lot of bidding space for the opponents.

ZOOM

Some players also have added a jump to 3 ♣ over a minor suit bid to show the other minor and a 5-card spade suit, because this is the only scenario not covered by Michaels and the Unusual No Trump. This is called Modified Michaels, and the opponents must be alerted that's it's not a standard bid.

The Hand Not Covered

- Your RHO bid 1 ♣.

- Now you're stuck. None of the Michaels bids or Unusual No Trump will show this hand.

- Overcalling 1 ♠ is your best bet here.

- This is the type of hand that prompted the development of the Modified Michaels bid.

Two-Suited Summary

- Cue bidding a minor shows two 5-card majors.

- Cue bidding a major shows 5 cards in the other major and an unspecified 5-card minor.

- Bidding 2NT shows 5 cards in the two lowest unbid suits.

OVERCALLS

VULNERABILITY
You have to know how to score in order to deal with interference

Now that you know players will be jumping into the bidding with fewer than 13 points, you can also surmise that your bidding is going to be getting a little more complicated.

When both pairs have entered the bidding, not only do you have to work harder to find your suit fit with your partner, but you also have to worry about how high to bid. Should you compete and bid up higher than you were planning or should you let the defense have it and set them? In order to really be able to figure out which you're going to do, you have to have a good handle on the scoring, and especially vulnerability. Whether or not you are vulnerable is going to make all the difference in the world.

If one pair only is bidding, then vulnerability doesn't come into play. Bid as accurately as you can.

Vulnerability Visual

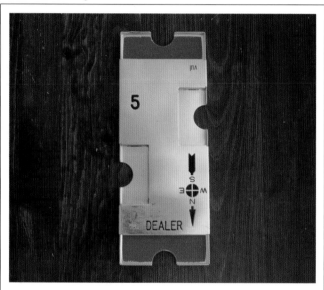

- Here's a duplicate board where the north/south (NS) pair is vulnerable and the east/west (EW) pair is not vulnerable.

- Different boards mark vulnerability in different ways, but this one is very common.

- Not only is it written on top of the board, but the card slots are color coded, too. Red for vulnerable.

The Auction

- This is the auction so far.

- North opened with 1 ♦. East jumped in with 1 ♥. South bid 1 ♠. West bid 2 ♥. North bid 2 ♠.

- Both sides have found their fit. Who is going to win the bid?

If, however, both pairs are bidding, you should look to the vulnerability to see how aggressive you should be with your bidding. If you're vulnerable, be less aggressive. If you're not vulnerable, be more aggressive.

Many times a nonvulnerable pair will make a very aggressive bid against a vulnerable pair, with the expectation of not making the contract. Because the penalty is relatively low, compared to the penalty for the other pair, this might keep the vulnerable pair out of a good contract. See the hands below for an example of this type of strategy.

ZOOM

My students have observed that this type of bridge seems sort of "mean" or "unfair." It may seem odd at first, but playing with the score is just as important as learning the bidding, the play, or the defense. It's all part of the game.

East's Hand

- East only has 11 points and west responded with a weak bid of 2 ♥.

- However, now the NS pair has a suit fit, it's time to be aggressive.

- If NS makes 2 ♠, they get 110 points. Because they're not vulnerable, EW can go down two tricks and still get a better score (-100 instead of -110).

- East should jump to 4 ♥ to make the decision hard for NS.

South's Hand

- After east jumps to 4 hearts, south is in a bind. She only has 7 points, and she's vulnerable.

- She knows the opponents are probably in over their heads, but if she bids 4 ♠, and they go down 2, that's -200 points.

- She has to pass. Her partner has another chance to bid if her hand happens to be stronger.

DEALING WITH INTERFERENCE

THEY TOOK MY BID
How do you respond when the opponents take your bid?

Sometimes when you're bidding, you get stuck in the uncomfortable situation of having the opponents take your bid. You have to have some tools for dealing with this. A lot depends on where you are in the bidding and what the bid actually meant.

If you're in the overcall seat, you should generally be quiet. Let's say the opponents bid 1 ♠ and you're sitting there with five spades and 13 points. Even though you were going to

say 1 ♠, there really is no point now. There are only three possible spades left in the deck, and the odds of your partner having all three (and therefore having a fit with you) are slim. Not only that, but even if you do have a fit, you'll have an awful 5–0 split from your opponents. Basically, you're relieved that they made the 1 ♠ bid, not you. You should pass and let them struggle to find their fit.

Overcall Seat

- Your right hand opponent (RHO) just bid 1 ♥. You have 14 points and had also planned to bid 1 ♥. What now?

- You have to pass. You have no other suit, and you don't want to be in hearts now that you know the player on your right also has 5.

- Even if your partner has three hearts and you have a fit, that means that you'll find yourself with a 5–0 trump split.

One No Trump

- Your partner bid 1 ♠. You were all set to say 1NT, but then the bidder before you jumped in with a 1NT bid of her own.

- How do you show your 8 points now? The answer is you don't. Play defense.

- Your partner has at least 13 points, you have 8. That makes 21 points, and the opponents only have 19. Who's most likely to get tricks in a no trump contract?

170

If the opponent's bid was an artificial bid (see the third example below), it gets a little trickier. In this case, you might have a fit with your partner, but you have no way of showing it without getting up too high. This is something you're going to have to work out with your partner. Some partnerships like to double the opponent's artificial bid. It shows support for the suit, but the inability to get up too high. Others like to pass and possibly compete later, depending on what the opponents bid.

They Bid Michaels

- In this case, your partner bid 1 ♥, and the next player bid 2 ♥—a Michaels bid showing five spades and five of a minor.

- You wanted to bid 2 ♥. If you bid 3 ♥ now, your partner might take you for more points.

- Some players use a double bid to show heart support and weaker points. You should discuss this with your partner.

An Inconvenient Minor

- You were all set to open 1 ♣, but that's exactly what your RHO bid.

- You know they probably don't have real clubs, but you can't bid your clubs without it sounding like a Michaels cue bid.

- Pass for now. If the bid comes around to you again, you can bid the clubs.

BALANCING SEAT
Force them higher and protect your partner

Once someone opens the bidding, everyone at the table gets stuck with a label. The first person is the opener. The next is the overcaller, and the third is the responder. The fourth player has a few different names, however, depending on how the bid goes. If the overcaller bid, then the fourth player is the advancer. If both the overcaller and the responder pass, however, the fourth is called the "balancing seat."

The balancing seat describes the player whose pass would end the auction, especially after minimal bidding. So for instance, let's say the bidding went 1 ♠, pass, pass. A third pass would end the auction and leave the opponents in a very simple easy bid to make.

As you just learned, there are times when your partner might be sitting in the overcall seat with 13 points, but for

One No Trump

- Your left hand opponent (LHO) bid 1 ♦, followed by two passes, and now it's your bid.

- You borrow a king, making 16 points.

- You can stop the diamonds, and with the borrowed three points, you have between 15 to 17 points.

- Bid 1NT.

Double

- Your LHO bid 1 ♥, followed by two passes and now it's your bid.

- You borrow a king, making 13 points.

- You don't have a 5-card suit, but you are short in hearts and can support the other three suits.

- Double.

whatever reason, he can't make a bid. You also know that the responder has fewer than 6 or he would have bid something. Because of that, you're going to want to make every effort to make a bid in the balancing seat.

A good rule of thumb is to borrow 3 points from your partner (many people refer to this as "borrowing a king"). If his 3 points gives you a bid, then go ahead and make that bid. You might bid a 5-card suit, you might bid no trump—if the opener has your suit—or you might double. If none of those are an option, or if you still don't have enough points with the extra 3, then go ahead and pass.

Don't forget to "give" the 3 points back. In other words, don't overvalue your hand. You were just borrowing the points to make a bid.

One Spade

- Your LHO bid 1 ♥, followed by two passes, and now it's your bid.

- You borrow a king, making 11 points.

- You have a 5-card suit, and 11 points is good enough to make an overcall bid.

- Bid 1 ♠.

Pass

- Your LHO bid 1 ♦, followed by two passes, and now it's your bid.

- You borrow a king, making 9 points.

- Even though you have a 5-card spade suit, you really don't have enough points. Your suit quality is poor.

- Pass. Chances are that the opponent has a big hand.

OVER NO TRUMP
Figure out a plan of action when your opponents interfere over your no trump bid

When one player in a partnership opens in 1NT, the chances of finding the exact right contract go up tremendously. With transfers and Stayman at their disposal, players are able to perfectly define their hands.

Because of this, interfering after a 1NT bid can be especially effective. Not only does it take up bidding space, it can also create confusion.

For instance, let's say your partner bids 1NT, and the next player bids 2 ♦. What does your 2 ♥ bid mean now? Is it hearts or is it a transfer to spades? What if you had two 4-card majors? How would you show that? Partnerships need to come to an agreement as to how they are going to handle

Three Spades

- Your partner bid 1NT and then the opponents jumped in with 2 ♦.

- Even though you could still do a transfer to spades, systems are off now and your bid is natural.

- Bid 3 ♠, not 2 ♠, to force your partner to game, either in 3NT or 4 ♠.

Two Spades

- Your partner bid 1NT and then the opponents jumped in with 2 ♦.

- This is the same shape as the last hand but with far fewer points.

- Bid 2 ♠ and hope that your partner will know enough not to bid on.

interference over no trump, because opponents are going to try to jump in whenever possible.

Many people play that systems are off over no trump interference. Some players use conventions. Some players use something called a "mirror double" or "They stole my bid double." Other players like to save that double for penalty. There are valid arguments for all of these, but you need to just be in agreement with your partner.

For your level, I recommend that you play that systems are off once there is interference. Every bid is natural. Knowing that, you need to jump a level when you bid a suit if you want to ensure that your partner knows that you're interested in game.

Double?

- Double is another bid you have to agree on. Is double for penalty or takeout?

- With this hand, it would be nice to have double be for takeout if the opponents bid 2 ♣.

- It would also be nice to have it be for penalty if they bid one of the majors.

- You need to choose.

Vulnerability Counts

- Take a look at the vulnerability on this one.

- If you're vulnerable and the opponents interfere, then you should jump right to 3NT.

- You'll rack up 600+ points.

- If, however, you're not vulnerable, then a double seems in order. You might get a lot more than 400 points whether they're vulnerable or not.

CAPPALLETTI
One method of interfering over an opponent's no trump

Now that you've learned how annoying it is to have someone interfere with your no trump bidding, you're going to have to make an effort to interfere yourself.

The first way to do it would be with natural bidding. If you overcall a suit over 1NT, you would have at least 5 cards in that suit with at least 10 points. Or you might have 6 cards with fewer points.

But what if you have a two-suited hand? We've already talked about how much more powerful two-suited hands are. You know you can interfere effectively, but Michaels doesn't work over a 1NT bid. Because of that, many players adopt a convention so that they can also interfere when they have two-suited hands, not just one-suited hands. There are many different conventions out there, but I'll just describe

Two ♣

- You have a 6-card spade suit. With natural bidding you would overcall 2 ♠ here.

- With Cappalletti, you bid 2 ♣, implying one long suit.

- If the opponents don't bid, your partner says 2 ♦ to keep the bidding open.

Two ♦

- Over a 1NT bid, you bid 2 ♦ with this hand if you play Cappalletti.

- If you don't, you would probably be reluctant to interfere, since you don't have the points to make an overcall.

- After your 2 ♦ bid, your partner would pick her better major.

176

one. Once you get more comfortable adding conventions to your repertoire, then you can do some research and figure out which one you like best.

The Cappalletti convention was invented by Mike Cappalletti. If you play this convention, there are six possible interfering bids that you can make after your opponent makes a 1NT bid:

double: for penalty, you have either a lot of points or a long suit to run.

2 ♣: I have one long suit, not necessarily clubs.

2 ♦: I have two 5-card majors.

2 ♥: I have five hearts and five of a minor.

2 ♠: I have five spades and five of a major.

2NT: I have two 5-card minors.

Two ♥

- Over a 1NT bid, you would bid 2 ♥ with this hand if you play Cappalletti.

- If you bid naturally, you would be torn.

- Do you bid the 6-card minor or do you bid the 5-card major? Either way, you should definitely interfere.

Double

- The opponents bid 1NT, and they are vulnerable. You are not.

- It might be tempting to steal the bid in spades, but start by doubling. You are highly likely to set the opponents by several tricks, which would get you a higher score.

- If the opponents switch to something else, then you can bid your spades.

177

OVER A PREEMPT
When the opponents start high, your choices are limited

One of the reasons that players make a preemptive bid, either on the two level or the three level, is to steal the bid when they have a long suit. The other reason is to take up a lot of the opponents' bidding room. If you're weak, it stands to reason that the opponents have some points. However, if you start at the two or three level, many of their bids will be impossible to make.

So how do you deal with it when it happens to you? There are several options you have, with the takeout double being the most likely one. If the opponents have a long suit, it stands to reason that you'll be short in it. A double lets you find out about your partner's suit. If you have a lot of points, then it also lets you find out something about your partner's hand before you place the contract.

Double

- The opponents jumped to 3 ♥. You only have a bare opener, but your shape is good for a double.

- Go ahead and take the risk that your partner might not have points but will be forced to bid.

- Double. Your partner must answer, and your partnership will get back into the bidding.

Bid Your Suit

- Again, the opponents bid 3 ♥.

- Bid your spade suit rather than doubling, because you have five in that suit.

- You hope that your partner will support it and that she has points.

If you don't have a lot of points or you aren't short in the opponent's suit, then you have to hope for a suit to bid yourself. If you have one, then go ahead and bid it.

If you have neither suit nor points, then you'll have to pass, hoping that perhaps your partner will be the one jumping into the bidding.

Double

- Again, the opponents bid 3 ♥.

- This hand looks exactly like the last one, shapewise, but it has a few more points.

- Double works here, because you want to find out something about your partner's hand.

- You're pretty sure you'll be heading to game, but you need to know where.

Pass

- Again, let's assume the opponents bid at the three level.

- This is a tricky hand. You might have a chance to make game if your partner has a few points, but you don't really have a good bid.

- A double is chancy. If your partner doesn't have points or a long suit, you really don't have enough of either to compensate.

- I'd pass.

POINTS ARE NOT EQUAL
The simple point count system is not so simple after all

Charles Goren, one of the most famous players ever to grace the game of bridge, revolutionized the way bridge was played in the fifties and sixties. Rather than bidding on pure gut instinct, he came up with the point evaluation system that many players use today: 4 points for an ace, 3 points for a king, 2 for a queen, and 1 for a jack.

While most people will agree that this point system does give a fairly accurate assessment of hand strength, there are others who've made it their business to tweak the system a little bit more. And there are still others who've thrown the entire system out the window.

Nonetheless, these other systems require a conceptual mastery of bridge that just isn't possible with beginners. So I encourage you to embrace the point count system for now,

Scattered Points

- This hand has 14 points and a 5-card major, so you should definitely open it with 1 ♠.

- Nonetheless, the points are scattered and a lot are from queens and jacks.

- I would not be aggressive with this hand.

Concentrated Points

- Compare this 14-point hand to the last one.

- Wouldn't you rather have this one?

- Same points, but this hand inspires much more confidence.

180

but by reading this chapter, you'll be able to make educated decisions based on what "type" of points you actually have.

To simplify, you should know that aces are slightly undervalued and that queens and jacks are slightly overvalued (kings are perfect) in this point count system. So if your points are mostly in kings and aces, then your hand might be a little stronger than the actual point count. If, however, your points are in queens and jacks, then the strength of your hand might be a little less than it shows numerically.

Additionally, if your points are in your long suits, you are better off than if your points are in your short suits. Also, if your points are grouped together rather than being scattered through all four suits, you again are better off. This rethinking of your points is especially important when you have a hand that's on the edge of a bid, such as a 10-point or a 12-point hand.

Quacky Hand

- Your partner bid 1 ♥.

- You have 8 points and heart support, so you respond 2 ♥.

- When your partner invites you to game, do you go?

- This is not a strong 8-point hand. I'd pass.

Ace/King Combo

- Same thing as before.

- Your partner bids 1 ♥, you respond 2 ♥, showing your support and your 8 points.

- You have the exact same heart support, but this time the other 7 points are an ace/king combo—much more helpful.

- Your solid club suit offers some good possibilities.

12-POINT HANDS
When your hand is close to opening

You pick up your hand, sort your cards, fan it, and discover that you have 12 points. Darn it. Close to opening but not quite. Should you open it anyway? After all, the 13 points to open is just a guideline, not a rule.

The answer is yes, most of the time.

Taking what you now know about point counts, you may want to be more aggressive and open your 12-point hands.

Are your points mostly in aces and kings or are they in queens and jacks? Are the points concentrated or scattered? This could influence whether you open or pass.

Even more important than the type or concentration of your points, though, is your shape. Long suits or two-suited hands tend to earn a player more tricks than flat hands that have three or four in every suit. The only time a flat hand

Twelve-Point Hand

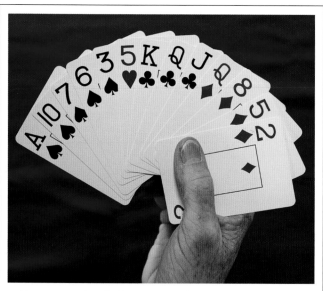

- Most competitive bridge players open most 12-point hands.

- The points aren't concentrated in your two suits, which would be best, but you do have two bids.

- Go ahead and open this 1 ♠.

Another 12-Point Example

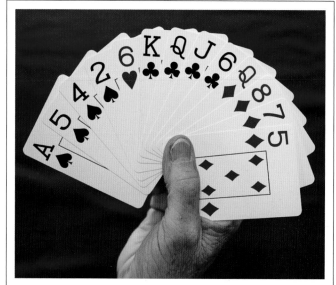

- Here are the same points, but different shape.

- But again, you have two bids, so it's a good 12-point hand to open.

- Begin by bidding 1 ♦. If your partner bids 1 ♥, you bid 1 ♠. If she bids 1 ♠, you bid 2 ♠.

is valuable is when you're in no trump. And if you're in no trump, then you better have those high cards to earn you some tricks. With only 12 points in your hand, you can't make that claim very easily.

A good rule of thumb is to look to see if you have two good bids. Can you bid a minor and then a 4-card major? Can you bid a major and then a 4-card minor? Even better, do you have two 5-card suits? If you have two suits, then it's worth opening a 12-point hand.

<table>
<tr><td>

Don't Open

</td><td>

Different 12 Points

</td></tr>
</table>

- Here are the same points again.

- You can open it 1 ♦, but where do you go from there?

- You don't have a 4-card major, so you'll probably end up in no trump. If your partner only has 6 points, you're playing 1NT with 18 points versus a pair with 22 points.

- You should pass to begin with.

- This hand has a different set of 12 points, but you can still see how the same concept applies.

- You have two suits, so you have two bids.

- The two suits you have are terrible, but your shape is interesting enough to make a bid with this 12-point hand worthwhile.

RULE OF 20
A tool to help you open hands with good shape but marginal point count

There are some hands that are just screaming to be opened because they have such good shape. However, if you rely solely on point count, you'll find yourself sadly passing all these hands. Or, if you happen to have a long suit, you'll bid your hand preemptively and continually find yourself under-bidding. Neither is a satisfactory way to play bridge.

As we've seen it's easier to be the opener than the overcaller. If there's any way you can open your hand, you should go for it. Not only will you and your partner communicate better, but your opponents will have a harder time describing their hands. And besides, who doesn't want to bid when they have the opportunity. It's part of the reason we play the game.

One Long Suit

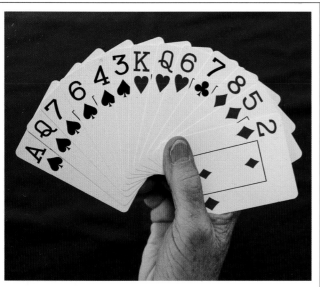

- This hand only has 11 points.

- Do you open this hand as a weak two bid, bidding 2 ♠, or do you open it as a 1 ♠ bid?

- Use the rule of 20.

- Eleven high card points plus the length of the two longest suits: 6+3 = 9. 11+9 = 20.

- This hand should be opened 1 ♠.

More Dramatic Example

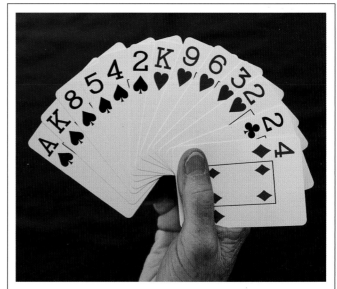

- This hand only has 10 points.

- Use the rule of 20: a 6-card suit plus a 5-card suit (6+5 = 11) added to your 10 high card points. (11+10 = 21).

- You see that it's actually a good opening hand, rather than a possible weak two bid.

184

A well-respected bridge expert named Marty Bergen was responsible for introducing the bridge world to the rule of 20. It's a way of evaluating your hand to include shape with your high card points. First you add up your high card points. If you're at 13, go ahead and bid. If you have fewer than 13 points, however, then use the rule of 20 to see if you should open that hand.

The rule of 20: Add the number of your high card points to the length of your two longest suits. If all three numbers added together is 20 or higher, then you should open that hand. In other words, if you have 12 points, a 5-card suit, and 4-card suit, you add 12+5+4, which equals 21 points. This hand should definitely be opened.

The rule of 20 values points and shape together. However, there is a caveat. Don't get so caught up with the "rule" that you forget the good advice from the previous section. Remember to also look at the quality of your points and where they're located.

Less Dramatic Example

- This hand has 12 points.

- There are no long suits, but there are still plenty of opportunities for you and your partner to find a suit fit.

- Use the rule of 20: a 4-card suit plus a 4-card suit (4+4 = 8) added to your 12 high card points. (8+12 = 20).

- Open this hand with 1 ♣.

Ignore the Rule

- Here's a hand that technically gets to the rule of 20.

- It has 11 high card points and a 5-card suit and a 4-card suit. (11+5+4 = 20).

- However, your points are all scattered.

- There are times when you have to use your instincts and realize that this probably doesn't match the intent of the convention.

- You should pass this hand.

10 POINTS
Using your partner's bid to help you place your bid

So now you've learned how to deal with "bubble hands" when you are the opener. But there are going to be lots of other bubble hands that come up in other situations. Do you have enough for game? Enough for slam? How high do you raise your partner? These all depend on the quality of your hand.

Ten-point hands are tricky hands when you're the responder. Many players think a simple raise is 6 to 9 points. An equal number of players will tell you it's 6 to 10 points. Many players will like 1NT to be 6 to 10 points. Others only like that over a minor. Over a major, they like 6 to 9. Sometimes a double raise with 10 points can be a disaster. Sometimes it's all you need to get to a tricky game.

Because of this, you should evaluate 10-point hands with the same care that you use to evaluate other bubble hands.

The 10-Point Hand

- This hand is neither weak nor strong.

- Reevaluate your hand once you hear your partner's bid to see which way to push it.

- Your partner opens 1 ♠.

- You don't have a fit and you don't have much else.

- Devalue and bid 1NT.

A Different 10-Point Hand

- Your partner opened 1 ♥, and you have this hand.

- This is an entirely different 10-point hand. Even though you don't have a fit yet, this hand is stronger.

- With this hand, a bid of 2 ♦ is reasonable and much better than a 1NT bid.

There isn't a clever "Rule of X" to help you figure out which 10-point hands are good and which are bad, but the same thoughts of shape and distribution of points apply.

When your points come from aces and kings, the hand is stronger than when they come from queens and jacks. When the honors in your hand are touching honors in one suit, rather than scattered honors throughout, they are more valuable.

And finally, use shape to help push you one way or the other. If you have an extra trump with a few singletons or doubletons, then your hand is dramatically stronger than one that is completely balanced.

With Support

- Your partner opened 1 ♠.

- You have the choice to bid 2 ♠ or 3 ♠ when you have 10 points.

- Look at your hand. The 10 points are scattered and lousy, and you only have three-card support.

- Bid 2 ♠.

Better Support

- Again, your partner opened 1 ♠.

- The shape is the same as the last hand and, like the last hand, you have 10 points. You can bid either 2 ♠ or 3 ♠.

- In this case, the quality of your points is much better.

- Bid 3 ♠.

NO TRUMP GAMBLES

The desire to avoid playing in a minor frequently puts you in a risky no trump bid

Bubble hands with no trump present an entirely different set of circumstances. If you have a long suit, it definitely pays off in no trump as it would with a suit contract, but it also necessarily entails a short suit somewhere else. In other words, it's a bit of a gamble.

Most players take that gamble when their long suit is a

minor. However, if the long suit is a major, then the points are similar enough that the player will make an effort to stay in his long suit. You need 11 tricks to make game in a minor and only 9 tricks to make game in no trump—that is what makes the no trump route with a long minor suit so tempting. Even if you can make 11 tricks easily, you can probably make 10

Opening Unconventionally

- This hand has 2 double-tons—generally a big no-no for opening 1NT.

- However, because they're both good doubletons, because you have 17 high card points, and because your partner can be so specific with her hand, a 1NT bid might be worth a gamble.

Another Odd Opener

- Again, you have two doubletons with this hand.

- This time they're not even two good doubletons.

- However, you have a running six-card club suit—a guarantee of 6 tricks. You'll get one more with the spades, so you just need two from your partner.

- It's worth the gamble to open 1NT.

or 11 in no trump too, resulting in a higher score and again making the no trump contract the better bid.

As you can see from the examples below, there are times when no trump seems like a decent gamble. Opening or responding with no trump with these types of hands won't always pay off, but it will work in your favor more often than not.

Responding to No Trump

- Your partner opened 1NT.

- You can't bid a transfer or Stayman because you don't have a major.

- Normally in this situation—with 9 points and no major to talk about—you should bid 2NT and invite.

- With this great club suit, however, you should gamble with 3NT.

No Points

- Your partner opened 1 ♥.

- You only have 6 points, so you can't bid your club suit.

- However, because you have that great club suit, a bid of 1NT is worth the gamble.

SLAM WITHOUT POINTS
Once again shape can be so much more powerful than points

An Unusual Slam

The general point guideline for slam is 33 points for a small slam and 37 for a grand slam. Nonetheless, we all know of slams that have the requisite number of points and fail or ones that are bid quite shy of points that make it because the cards line up correctly.

The first type of hand is one you can play and forget about. Everyone else will be there, and most people won't make it. You don't have to beat yourself up. Look at the second example. This is exactly the type of frustrating hand where this happens.

The first example, though, is completely different. There aren't nearly enough points for slam, yet it's going to make it every time.

Here are a few hands that show how easily slam can be made as long as the shape of the hand cooperates. However, they're not all easy to bid.

- The opening spade bidder has 13 high card points.

- The responder has 10.

- Together, they technically don't even have the 26 points for game, yet this hand will easily make a small slam.

- If the defense doesn't find the club lead, the declarer can take all 13 tricks by dumping the clubs on the dummy's nice diamonds.

- Shape can make all the difference.

Look at the hands shown on this page. In the first one, the declarer has an 8-card trump suit and two singletons. In his hand alone, he can be pretty confident of 9 tricks off the top, barring any bad trump splits. This slam might be hard to find, however, if he starts the bidding with 1 ♥. If he starts the bidding with 2 ♣, he's going to find out that his partner has a pretty strong hand, which might make him more hopeful. In addition, the partner is not going to have any idea that shape is driving the bid, not points, so that player will eagerly head to slam.

Matching Hands

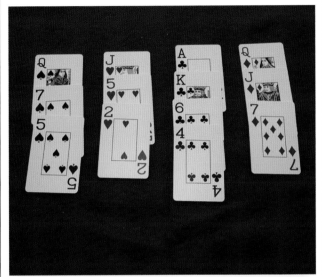

- In this hand, the opposite is true.

- One hand has 13 points, and the other has 22 points.

- No matter which one opens, the other will know they have plenty of points for slam.

- Unfortunately their shape matches perfectly. There is no long suit in either hand to pitch the losers from the other hand.

- Their points also fall on each other. While you'd like to think you could get 4 tricks from the spade or diamond suit, since you have the AKQJ in both, it's impossible. You can only get 3 tricks, because the high cards fall on each other.

REEVALUATION

Once you've found your fit, now you can take a look at your hand's features

We've talked about how some hands are stronger than others, just because of the shape of the hand or the fact that the points are concentrated in one suit. There's another factor that comes into play when you're trying to figure out how high to bid. It's your fit with your partner.

If you and your partner have found a suit fit, then other features in your hand suddenly become more valuable. For instance, let's say you have a singleton spade and 9 points. When your partner opens 1 ♠, your singleton looks pretty terrible. You bid 1NT.

Now let's say your partner opens 1 ♥. You have four hearts, when he only really needs three for a fit, plus you have a

Quick Fit

- You bid 1 ♠, and your partner says 2 ♠.

- You know she has 6 to 9 points, and you have 18 high card points.

- Do you invite to game or go?

- Now that you know you have a fit, you can count your singleton club for 2 more points. You should go right to game.

Responding with a Fit

- This hand has 8 high card points, but it seems to be stronger than just its 8 points. How strong is it?

- Your partner bid 1 ♥, so you have a fit, plus you have an extra heart. Give yourself a point for that.

- You also have a single-ton—2 points—and a doubleton—1 more point.

- You're now up to 12 points. You can jump to three hearts in support.

singleton spade. Now your hand looks great! The suit fit made all the difference.

Because of this, you can give yourself extra points, once you find your fit. For every card over the expected amount in the trump suit, give yourself 1 point. For every void, give yourself 3 points; for every singleton, give yourself 2 points; and for every doubleton, you can give yourself 1 point.

This is called reevaluating your hand, and it can help you get to game when you don't actually have the high card points.

Responding—No Fit

- Your partner bid 1 ♥, and this is your hand.

- It has the same 8 points as the last hand, but the shape is different.

- This time your singleton is in your partner's suit.

- Bid 1NT. You don't have enough points to bid your diamonds.

No Shortness

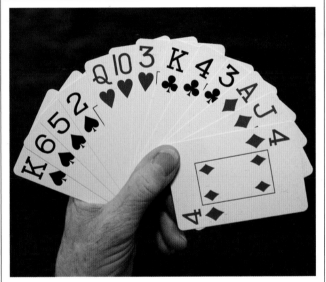

- You opened 1 ♣ with this hand.

- Your partner bid 1 ♥, you bid 1 ♠. Your partner then bid 2 ♠.

- Do you go on? No.

- You found your spade fit, but this hand offers nothing extra.

NO FIT
Take your hand down a notch when you can't find a fit

The upside of reevaluation is that you can sometimes reach a game without the points. The downside is that sometimes reevaluation can work in the opposite direction. If you don't have the fit, your hand is suddenly worth a whole lot less.

Be careful not to give yourself points for shortness until you find your fit. Too many times players will open the bidding because they have a void, thinking it makes their hand so much stronger, and then their partner has nothing but that suit that they're void in.

Let's say you have a 10-point hand with four spades, no hearts, five diamonds and four clubs. Some players see that void and give themselves 3 points right off the bat, bringing them to 13 and they open the hand. (Notice, by the way, that this did not meet the rule of 20 requirements either.)

Responding

- Your partner opened 1 ♥, and you have this hand.

- Suddenly your singleton heart doesn't look so hot.

- Bid 1NT. You can't bid your club suit, because your hand just isn't strong enough.

A Void

- You opened 1 ♥ with this hand.

- It's a mere 13 pointer, but it has a void, so it's full of potential.

- Then your partner bids 2 ♠ (of course).

- You bid your diamond suit now, and your partner rebids his spades. Your hand is looking weaker and weaker, and now your contract is up to the three level in spades! Not good.

194

Then disaster strikes. They open 1 ♦. Their partner bids 1 ♥, they bid 1 ♠. Their partner bids 2 ♥. They try 3 ♣, and their partner goes to 3NT. Now what? The two of them are in a contract where the high card wins, and instead of the 13 points one partner was counting on from the other's hand, he'll only be getting 10.

Your void *is* likely to be valuable, and there's a good chance you'll be able to jump in the bidding, but with a hand like that you should pass at first.

Rule of 20

- Because of the rule of 20, you opened 1 ♥ with this hand.

- Your partner bid 1 ♠.

- You're relieved he didn't bid clubs, but you're not sure that he has 5 ♠.

- You bid 2 ♦. He jumps to 3NT.

- You should correct to 4 ♠. Even if you're short one spade, you're better off in a suit than in no trump.

Responding

- Your partner opened 1 ♦, and you have this hand.

- You answered with 1 ♥, and your partner responded 1 ♠.

- Instead of saying 1NT at this point, which would make your hand weaker, you should support his diamonds to capitalize on your void.

195

REVERSES
Use a simple bidding trick to show more points

When you are the opener and have two suits to bid of equal length, you bid the higher one first. Then, if you need to offer the second one, you can bid it and your partner can correct to your first suit at the same level.

If you had done this bidding in reverse, then if your partner wanted to correct to your first bid suit, she would have to go up a level. Unless you have a ton of points, this is not a wise thing to do. But now let's flip that last statement around. If you DO have a lot of points, then that is exactly what you need to do. This is a way of showing your partner what a big hand you have without having to jump. It's called a "reverse," because it's the reverse of what would normally be the prudent bid.

There is one glaring exception to this rule. When you begin

Classic Reverse

- You opened 1 ♣ with this hand.

- Your partner then responded with 1 ♥. You're tempted to jump to 2NT to show your points and your balanced hand, but those spades are worrisome.

- Bid 2 ♦ instead. This is a reverse and shows your shape and points.

- If your partner has spades stopped, he can go to no trump now.

Common Reverse Mistake

- Again, you opened 1 ♣ with this hand, and your partner bid 1 ♥.

- The shape is exactly the same, but the points are different.

- With this hand, you have to be careful not to bid your diamonds now.

- Bidding 1NT is probably your best gamble.

with one of a minor and your partner says 1 ♥, you can say 1 ♠ without it being misconstrued as a reverse. This is normal bidding.

However, once you and your partner learn how to use reverses to show a big hand, you'll have to be careful that you don't use a reverse inadvertently.

Another Reverse Example

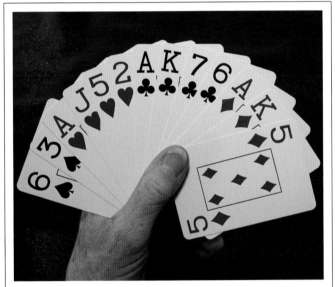

- You opened 1 ♣ with this hand.

- Your partner bid 1 ♠. By bidding 2 ♥ here, you are reversing and showing your 19 points.

- Your partner can either support either of your suits, rebid his suit if he has five, or go to 2 or 3NT, depending on points.

Not a Reverse

- You opened 1 ♣ with this hand.

- Your partner bid 1 ♥.

- Bidding 1 ♠ here is not a reverse. Yes, this suit is higher than your original suit, but your partner is able to make a weak bid to return to your first suit if he chooses.

THIRD HAND BIDDING

Once you've found your fit, you can take a look at your hand's features

When the bidding begins with two passes, the player in the third seat might have some thinking to do. If she has an opening hand, there's nothing to worry about. She opens her hand as usual. If she has a very weak hand, there's also nothing to think about. But if she has an average hand—about 10 or 11 points—she might want to do a little gambling.

When you're sitting in the third seat holding an average hand after two passes, you can confidently assume that there are probably two scenarios. The first is that the hands are divided pretty equally. If there are 40 points in the deck, then each hand could theoretically have roughly 10 points and no one could open. In this case, you and your partner have as

Good Third Seat Bid

- You have 11 points. You can't quite get to the rule of 20, but you have a good suit.

- The other plus is that your suit is spades, so you really

take a lot of bidding space from your opponents.

- Bid 1 ♠ in the third seat.

Marginal Third Seat Bid

- This hand isn't quite as good. You have 10 points, and again you can't get to the rule of 20.

- You also don't take up a ton of bidding space with this bid.

- Nonetheless, it's excellent for lead direction, and you do have a good suit and a second bid.

- Bid 1 ♦.

much chance of winning half the tricks as the opponents, and if you get to pick the trump suit, then perhaps you'll win a few more. It's probably smart to jump in the bidding, even if you are a little on the light side.

The second scenario is that the fourth player has quite a few points and the points are not equally distributed. In this case, you might want to jump in the bidding as well. If she has a lot of points, she's going to want to bid, and your bid just might make her bid a little more difficult.

So, given that both scenarios seem to warrant a bid with a

light hand in that third seat, you probably are going to want to jump in the bidding if you find yourself in that situation.

Best to Pass

- This hand has 10 points, but again you can't get to the rule of 20.

- From the earlier chapters, you can see that this hand isn't a strong 10 points.

- Your suit also stinks with the queen as the only honor.

- It would be better to pass this one.

Third Seat Pitfalls

- You get too caught up in stealing the bid and open when you're too light.

- Your partner forgets that you opened light and counts on you for an opening hand, jumping to game.

- You're vulnerable, the opponents double for penalty and your partner has zero points.

A PASS IS OKAY

Just because you have the points to bid doesn't mean you should bid

If no one has bid, then your decision to open your hand or not is fairly straightforward. Do you have 13 points? If you don't, can you get to the rule of 20? If the answer to both of these is no, you pass. If it's yes, you bid.

Once someone has bid, however, your decision becomes more complicated. Let's say the opponents opened 1NT,

and you have 13 points but no suit. You don't really want to double, because that implies a penalty double and you're not sure at all if you can set them. What do you do? Pass. In the best case scenario your partner will have a nice balancing seat bid. At worst, you play defense. It's okay. You may be better off than the partnership who tried to grab the bid.

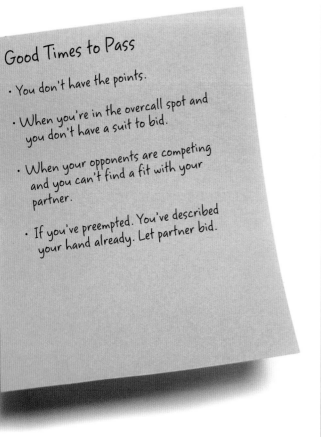

Good Times to Pass

• You don't have the points.

• When you're in the overcall spot and you don't have a suit to bid.

• When your opponents are competing and you can't find a fit with your partner.

• If you've preempted. You've described your hand already. Let partner bid.

Bad Spot

• Your right hand opponent (RHO) bid 1 ♦.

• You have 15 points. What do you bid here?

• Sadly, you have to pass. It's not a good double, you don't have a 5-card suit, and you can't say no trump, because you can't stop the diamonds.

Let's say your partner bids a suit, and you don't have it—either a singleton or a void. You also don't have any points. Again, it's okay to pass. Don't try to rescue your partner. If you're that weak, chances are your opponents will be trying to bid. And the last thing you want is to bid, give misinformation, and then find your partner rebidding his suit at a higher level.

Don't Compete

- You opened this rather ugly hand 1 ♣.

- Your partner bids 1 ♥, and your RHO bids 1 ♠.

- You raise to 2 ♥, followed by two passes, and then your RHO bids 2 ♠.

- You have no extras. You should pass. Let your partner compete if she has more.

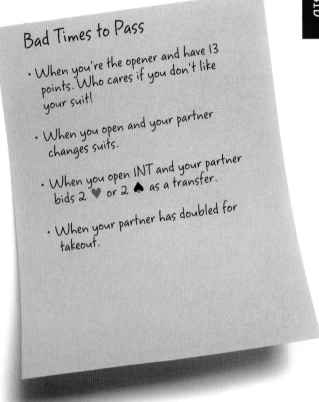

Bad Times to Pass

- When you're the opener and have 13 points. Who cares if you don't like your suit!

- When you open and your partner changes suits.

- When you open 1NT and your partner bids 2 ♥ or 2 ♠ as a transfer.

- When your partner has doubled for takeout.

DOUBLE FIT

If you have two 8-card suits between you, the value of your hand goes up

Minor Side Suit

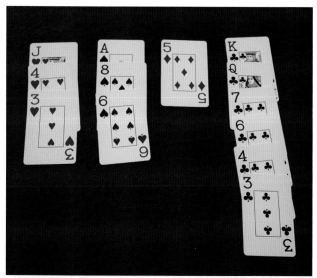

The more points you have, the more time you should take to explore your bid. The reason for exploring is twofold. First, you don't want to just jump to game and miss slam, and second, you may find out that you and your partner have a double fit.

A double fit is when you have two 8-card suits between the two hands. This doesn't always work to your advantage, but quite often it does. One of the suits can be trump, and one can be a nice side suit.

How do you pick which should be which? It's easy if one is a major and one is a minor. You should always take the major, purely because you'll get more points for taking the same number of tricks.

However, if they're both majors or both minors, which one is better? If the distribution is the same, it really doesn't matter. However, if you have one that's a 4–4 fit (which means

- You found your heart fit, but your partner opened this hand in clubs and repeated them, so you know he probably has six.

- You have 9 cards in the minor and only 8 in the major. Which do you choose?

- I hope you said the major. The minor will play out nicely as a side suit.

- Even though you don't quite have the points for game, you should take the gamble and go for it, because you know you have a nice double fit.

- If you look at this hand, you see that you can pull trump and then pitch your loser spade and your loser diamonds on the long club suit in the dummy.

- Even with the perfect defense, it makes 6 hearts, and here you only had 24 points between the two of you.

4 cards in one hand and 4 cards in the other hand) and one that's a 5–3 fit (5 cards in one hand and three in the other) or a 6–2 fit, then you want to choose the 4–4 fit for the trump suit. The imbalanced hand should be the side suit.

Here's why. Let's assume you pull trump. Now you're set to run your side suit. If you have the 4–4 fit as the side suit, then you don't get to pitch any losers. Every time you play that suit from one hand, you also play the same suit from the other hand. With the imbalanced hand, you get to throw off some losers as you run the suit from the long side.

When you have a 4–4 fit and get a bad trump split, it's never fun, but this is still the smart strategy.

Major Double Fit

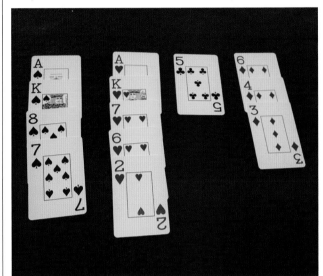

- In this case, you have a double fit in both major suits.

- Which do you pick?

- You pick the spades because it's the 4–4 fit and leave the hearts—the 5–3 fit—to be your side suit.

- So, now that you've chosen wisely, you've ended up in 6 ♠, gambling on the slam because you have the double fit.

- What's your strategy?

- Win the lead, no matter what it is. Trump 2 club tricks and then pull trump.

- Now run your hearts, pitching your two diamond losers on the long hearts in dummy.

203

OPENING HANDS

Try these bidding exercises to practice your skills

This chapter will help you practice your bidding. Each hand pictured here presents a bidding situation and some questions. Look at the pictures and questions first, before you read on.

Exercise 1. The opening bid for this hand is 1 ♣. Don't get tempted by that beautiful spade suit. If you open 1 ♠, your partner will count on you for five spades. If he has four spades,

he'll respond 1 ♠ when you open the club. If he doesn't have four spades, then you didn't want to be there anyway. If, however, your partner responds with 1 ♥, you may now bid 1 ♠. As long as it's your second suit, you only need four.

Exercise 2. I hope you picked the crummy suit over the good suit. Even though your diamonds are beautiful, you have to be accurate about the number of cards in your major suit.

Exercise 1

- In this hand, you have exactly 13 points.

- Your spade suit is beautiful, but you only have four of them.

- What is your opening bid?

Exercise 2

- In this hand, you have 17 points and two 5-card suits.

- One is a major and one is a minor.

- The major is terrible, and the minor is solid.

- Which do you pick?

By bidding 1 ♠, you tell your partner you have five spades. If you start with the diamond suit, and then say your spades, he'll never take you for five.

Exercise 3. If you're the opener and have two suits of the same length, you should always bid top down. First bid the higher one (the spades) and then at the next opportunity, you bid the lower one.

Exercise 4. Once you learn Stayman and transfer bids over a 1NT opener, you'll be thrilled with the accuracy and opportunity those bids provide. Because of this, I would open this hand 1NT every time. Occasionally I might get burned by my terrible spade holding, but more often than not, I'll end up in the perfect contract because it's so easy for my partner and me to communicate.

Exercise 3

- In this case, you have 13 points and both major suits.

- Your hearts are better than your spades.

- Does this matter?

- Which suit do you open first?

Exercise 4

- You have 15 points and a balanced hand.

- You also have a worthless spade doubleton and a 5-card minor.

- Do you bid 1NT or do you bid 1 ♦?

RESPONSES
Look at these problems to figure out how you would answer your partner

The hands on these two pages are all responding hands. What do you bid after your partner opens?

Exercise 5. Your partner opened 1 ♠. The weaker your hand, the faster you need to let your partner know that you have a trump fit. Since you only have 6 points, you should bid 2 ♠. Don't get distracted by your heart suit. You don't have

enough points to change suits on the two level, and since you already have a major suit trump fit, stick with that. Your hearts will be a lovely side suit.

Exercise 6. When you hear your partner bid a minor, your first responsibility is to come back with your 4-card major. In this case, you have both majors, so you go up the ladder,

Exercise 5

- Your partner has bid 1 ♠.

- Do you have a fit?

- How many points do you have in your hand?

- What is your bid?

Exercise 6

- Your partner has opened 1 ♦.

- What is your first responsibility as a responder when your partner bids a minor?

- Which suit do you bid?

telling her about the hearts first. Your bid is 1 ♥. If your partner has four hearts, she'll raise you. If she has four spades, she'll mention them, and then you will raise her. If she offers clubs, you correct back to diamonds. In all of these cases, you need to make an invitational bid, not a weak bid.

Exercise 7. Once your partner bids the spades as her second bid, you can be sure that she doesn't have five of them. With five of a major, she would have opened the major instead of the minor. Since you know you don't have a fit, go to 1NT. This is a weak bid in response, and it suits your balanced hand.

Exercise 8. This is also a 1NT bid. Bidding 1NT over a minor denies a 4-card major and describes a hand that is balanced with 6 to 10 high card points. That describes this hand perfectly.

Exercise 7

- Your partner bid 1 ♣.

- Your first response is easy. You bid 1 ♥, showing your 4-card major.

- Now your partner bids 1 ♠.

- What is your bid?

Exercise 8

- Your partner opened with 1 ♣.

- You have no 4-card major.

- You have no 5-card suit.

- You have 7 points.

- What do you bid?

OVERCALLS
Figure out what to bid when the opponents grab the opening spot

The hands on these two pages are all overcalls. Overcalls are much trickier than opening hands. It's not always clear cut and many of your possible bids go away. Here are some good examples. What do you bid here after your opponent opens?

Exercise 9. This is a perfect 1 ♠ overcall bid. You have at least five spades and at least 10 points. Your points are concentrated in the suit you're bidding, and if the opponents still end up with the bid, you've done a great job giving lead direction to your partner.

Exercise 10. Your overcall here is 1NT. You have a balanced hand with 15 to 17 points, and you can stop the opponent's suit. You could open 1NT without stoppers in every suit, but as soon as you're in the overcall position, you have to be able

Exercise 9

- Your right hand opponent (RHO) bid 1 ♣.

- You have 10 points.

- What is your bid?

Exercise 10

- Again, you are in the overcall seat, but this time your RHO bid 1 ♠.

- However, you don't have a 5-card suit to overcall.

- What do you bid?

to stop the opponent's suit, because that is exactly what his partner is going to lead.

Exercise 11. With this hand you have to pass. You can't bid no trump because you don't have enough points. And not only do you not have a 5-card suit, but you don't even have a 4-card suit, because the opponent already bid it. This is a hand where you play defense. You have points and a little something in every suit. The opponents may have trouble finding a successful contract.

Exercise 12. I hate overcalling with such a crummy suit, but

I would anyway in this case for a few reasons: You have 13 points, you have good shape, and you have an extra spade. Bid 1 ♠.

Exercise 11

- This hand is very similar to the last one except for one significant difference—you're missing the spade king. It's now a 10.

- How does this change the bidding?

- What is your bid now?

Exercise 12

- Once again, you're in the overcall seat.

- In this hand, your RHO has bid 1 ♥.

- What is your bid?

209

DOUBLES
A good bid for the overcaller who doesn't have a suit to bid

The hands on these two pages are examples where you should be thinking about a takeout double. Some are good double opportunities, and at least one is not a good double, though it may tempt you.

Exercise 13. Ideally, we want a double to have a singleton (or void) in the opponent's suit and four in every other suit. In this case, it's close but not perfect. Instead of four diamonds

and four clubs, you have three diamonds and five clubs. Nonetheless, double is still the best bid here. It's probably the only way you'll find a 4–4 heart fit.

Exercise 14. Tweaking one little card makes a huge difference sometimes. In this case, you don't want to double. If the opponent bids a major, a double should always promise four of the other major, because after all, that's your bidding goal.

Exercise 13

- Your right hand opponent (RHO) bid 1 ♠.

- If the 2 of clubs was a 2 of diamonds the double would be the clear bid.

- Is it still a good bid?

Exercise 14

- Again, your RHO bid 1 ♠.

- In this hand the hearts and the diamonds have been swapped.

- Does this make a difference in what you bid?

- What is your bid?

Because you don't have four of the other major, your bid here is just a 2 ♣ overcall.

Exercise 15. The shape of this hand is all wrong for a take-out double, but the hand is so strong that you should make one anyway. If the opponent has (roughly) 13 points (which you know because he opened), and you have 18 points, then there are only 9 points left for your partner and the other opponent. If you just bid 1 ♥ here, there's a really good chance you'll see it followed by three passes. That would be a tragedy. Double and then bid. Your partner should pick up

on the fact that you have a big hand.

Exercise 16. A takeout double is a great option here. You have both majors. Granted, one of them is a 5-card major and the other is a 4 card, but doubling gives you two chances to find a major fit.

Exercise 15

- Your RHO bid 1 ♣.
- What is your bid?

- You're void in clubs, plus you have 18 high card points.

Exercise 16

- Your RHO bid 1 ♣.
- What is your bid?

- You have exactly 13 points, and a 5-card suit, but your points are elsewhere.

DOUBLE RESPONSES
Your partner forced you to bid. Now what?

The hands on these two pages are for the partner of a doubler. If your partner doubles for takeout, there are a few things you need to keep in mind. See if you can remember them and get the answers right in this section.

Exercise 17. You absolutely should choose the hearts in this case. You might have a better diamond fit, but you want to be in a major if you can, and this is your only chance to get there. When your partner doubles a major, she's virtually guaranteeing four of the other major. If your partner, instead, has a big hand and bids something else, then you can show her the diamond suit.

Exercise 18. As much as you want to pass this hand, you need to respond with 2 ♦. If you pass, then the opponent is also likely to pass, and the contract will end at 1 ♠ doubled.

Exercise 17

- Your left hand opponent (LHO) bid 1 ♠.

- Your partner doubled for takeout.

- You have five diamonds and four hearts.

- What is your bid?

Exercise 18

- Your LHO bid 1 ♠.

- Your partner doubled for takeout.

- The next player passed.

- You have 1 point. What do you say now that it's your turn?

It's pretty easy to make 1 of anything, so they're likely to make their contract and now they get double the points to boot. You won't be misleading your partner, because she forced you to bid.

Exercise 19. In this case, the hearts are the obvious choice, but because your partner made a demand bid, you could have 0 points in your hand. You have to make sure that your partner knows that you have both hearts and points. Jump a level and bid 3 ♥, rather than just 2 ♥.

Exercise 20. In this case, you don't have the extra points, but you do have a huge heart suit. Take the gamble and jump all the way to game. Your partner promises an opening hand when she doubles, and you have the trump suit. Between the two of you, you should be able to make game.

Exercise 19

- Again, your LHO bid 1 ♠.
- What is your bid here?
- Your partner doubled for takeout.

Exercise 20

- Again, your LHO bid 1 ♠.
- What is your bid?
- Again, your partner doubled for takeout.

NO TRUMP RESPONSES

Master these bids, and soon they'll be among the easiest ones you can make

The hands on these two pages are all hands that have to respond after a 1NT bid.

Exercise 21. You don't have a 5-card major, so you're not going to do transfers, but you do have a 4-card major, so you want to use Stayman. Your first bid is 2 ♣. When your partner says 2 ♥, you've found your fit. Now you look at your points.

Knowing that your partner has at least 15, you add your 11 to that and know that you can be in game. Your next bid is to jump to 4 ♥. Don't bid 3 ♥, because then she has to guess at something that you already know. And what if she guesses wrong? If she responds with 2 ♦ instead of 2 ♥, you jump to 3NT.

Exercise 21

- Your partner bid 1NT.

- What is your first bid with this hand?

- When your partner says 2 ♥ after that what is your next bid?

- What would your bid be if she had said 2 ♦?

Exercise 22

- Your partner bid 1NT, and I'm assuming you're playing transfers.

- What is your first bid with this hand?

- When your partner says 2 ♥ after that, what is your next bid?

Exercise 22. Because you have a 5-card major, you bid 2 ♦ to transfer. She will say 2 ♥, and now you have to think about placing the contract. Do you have a heart fit? You're not sure, because she might only have two hearts. Do you have game-going points? Yes. Bid what you know. You know you have game, so go to game. Bid 3NT. Let your partner decide whether it should be in no trump or hearts.

Exercise 23. You have a 4-card major, so bid 2 ♣. Your partner now says 2 ♥. That is not your major, so you're going back to no trump. If your partner has the other major, she can then

correct to that. She knows you have at least one major, so if it's not hearts, it must be spades. Because you only have 9 points, bid 2NT. If your partner had said 2 ♠, you'd bid 3 ♠.

Exercise 24. Because you have neither a 5-card major nor a 4-card major, you want to stay in no trump. (You want nothing to do with minors, remember?) Do you have enough points for game? Yes. Bid game then, by saying 3NT.

Exercise 23

- Your partner bid 1NT.

- What is your first bid with this hand?

- When your partner says 2 ♥ after that, what is your next bid?

- What would your bid be if she had said 2 ♠?

Exercise 24

- Your partner bid 1NT.

- You can't do Stayman or transfers.

- What is your bid with this hand?

PLAYING COMPETITIVELY
Learn how to take your bridge game to a club or tournament

If you've learned how to play bridge at a bridge club, then you're probably already playing in a regular duplicate game, but if you're not, and you've fallen in love with this complicated game, your next step would be to take your game to a club or to a tournament.

Most clubs (and almost all tournaments) will have special games for novice players, so you can cut your teeth on duplicate bridge without a big intimidation factor getting in your way. You will be playing against less experienced players, and you will be given a tiny bit more slack for your possible unintended indiscretions.

Every sanctioned bridge game will have someone called a director. The director runs the game, makes sure the rotation is followed properly, and resolves any disputes that may arise.

KNACK BRIDGE FOR EVERYONE

Board Rotation

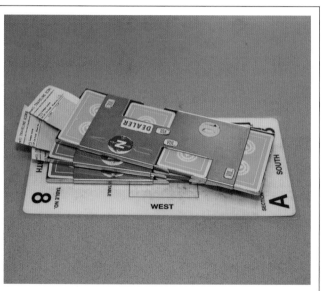

- The number of boards played during a session of bridge varies, depending on the level of play and the number of tables.

- Most open games are 24, 26, or 27 boards, divided up equally among the tables.

- Novice games tend to have fewer boards.

- The boards move down a table after they are played.

Table Rotation

- At a big bridge game, pairs either sit north/south or east/west.

- The north/south pairs stay at the same table for the whole game.

- The east/west players move up a table to play against a new north/south pair after each set of hands.

Feel free to ask the director for as much help as you need—not on the bidding, just on the logistics.

Some players get very resentful when the director is called, but it's absolutely the correct thing to do. With a fair ruling from the director, everyone can feel as if the issue has been resolved appropriately. If the players try to resolve something themselves, not only might it be resolved incorrectly (possibly resulting in a skewed score that affects the whole room), but one pair may end up feeling cheated.

Keeping Score

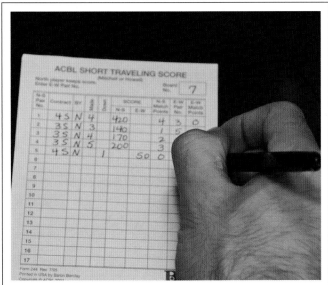

- Scores can be kept electronically, with a traveler, or with a pick up slip.

- The north player is responsible for entering the score.

- Everyone else at the table is responsible for making sure the score was entered correctly.

- Sit east/west your first time at a club or tournament so you can see how it's done.

Director, Please

- If you think anything is done improperly, be sure to ask the director to come resolve the question.

- Not only are you protecting yourself, but you're protecting the game's integrity for the other players in the room.

- Therefore, don't ever resent it when someone calls the director on you.

BIDDING
Keep a poker face while you're bidding regardless of the surprises that may come your way

Bridge is a unique card game. You're not out to manipulate the opponents. There's no bluffing like poker. The bidding has to be completely transparent to the defense. It's all about your skill and judgment as a bidder and player, and your ability to communicate effectively with the fifteen words you're given.

Even a pass might convey information. If you and your partner have found your heart fit, and the opponents compete with a spade bid, and then you agonize and agonize and take forever to bid, you're clearly sending your partner information that you're on the bubble and considering competing. If you bid, that's fine, but if you then pass, your partner can use

Don't Touch!

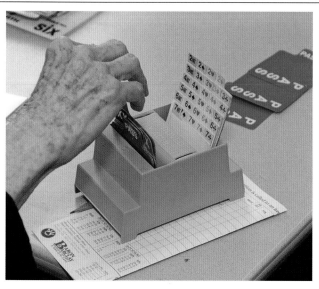

- Some players fiddle with the cards as they're trying to figure out what to bid.

- You would be surprised as to how much illegal (though unintended) information your partner can get by this behavior.

- Do all your thinking before you touch the bidding box.

Mechanical Error

- Sometimes you pull the wrong bid out of the box because your thumb caught the card below or the card you wanted slipped back into the bidding box.

- This is a correctable mistake as long as you catch it immediately.

- It's always safest to call the director, but most opponents will just let you correct a mechanical error.

that information to perhaps compete with a bid when it's her turn. And that's unethical.

The worst offense, however, is the extra chatter. There should be absolutely no talking. If you're playing with the bidding boxes, take that literally. If you have to talk to bid, you're allowed those fifteen words and that's it. Here are comments I hear all the time that just make me cringe:

"Well, I probably shouldn't bid this, but what the heck."

"We probably don't have it, but since we're not vulnerable, I'm stealing it back."

"I'm sure you're not going to know what I mean by this."

You get the general idea. Players who do this are cheating. In their mind it might be more of an apology or an explanation for crazy bidding, but it's cheating nonetheless. Keep quiet.

Bidding Error

- Other times you make a brain error, rather than a mechanical error. This cannot be changed.

- Do not attempt to correct it. Do not call the director.

- You also may not say anything that might communicate to your partner that you made a mistake.

- If you're lucky, you'll get another chance to bid, and then perhaps you can correct your mistake.

Partner's Bidding Error

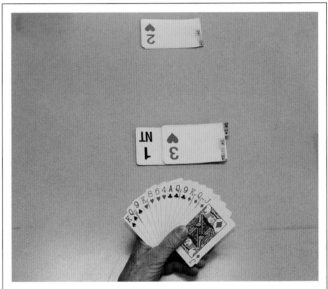

- Sometimes your partner might make a bidding error.

- One of the more common mistakes for beginners is forgetting the transfer bids.

- You cannot tell her that your bid was a transfer.

- You cannot sigh or moan or roll your eyes either.

THE DUMMY
More than just a pretty face

In social bridge at someone's home, being the dummy means getting a break. You might refresh your drink, chat with someone else, or just enjoy the play. You may ask to see your partner's hand before she actually plays it, or even go stand behind her and watch her play.

At duplicate bridge, the dummy actually has strict responsibilities and limitations and is an integral part of the game.

She is expected to stay at the table for the duration of the hand, playing her hand at the direction of the declarer.

She may not ever look at her partner's hand, and she certainly may never question the card that her partner has asked for. Your partner may have a very good reason for overtaking her king with your ace, or she might just be making a mistake, but you, as the dummy, are required to just follow her

Dummy Opportunity

- Being the dummy can be a great opportunity to improve your game.

- Because you don't have to concentrate on how to play the game, you can work on your card-counting skills and your bridge analysis.

- Try to figure out what is in every hand.

Keep Silent

- The dummy is called "dummy" for a reason. You are required to stay silent.

- You cannot ask for a review of the bidding or ask what a discard might mean.

- You cannot chat with other players at the table, which would be both annoying and distracting.

- And you may not ever question the card that your partner calls for, even if he's trumping his own ace.

direction to the letter without hesitation or questioning.

The one thing a dummy can do is protect her partner from a revoke. If spades are played, for instance, and the declarer does not follow suit with a spade, the dummy is allowed to say, "No spades, partner?" Defenders are allowed to say this to their partner's as well.

Noticing an Error

- Pay attention to any irregularities.

- If, however, you pick up on a revoke or some other indiscretion, you may not

say so until the very end of the hand.

- Do not interrupt the play if no one else has noticed.

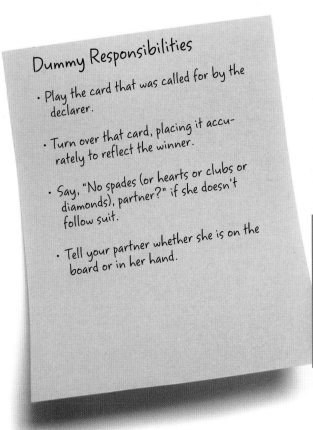

Dummy Responsibilities

- Play the card that was called for by the declarer.

- Turn over that card, placing it accurately to reflect the winner.

- Say, "No spades (or hearts or clubs or diamonds), partner?" if she doesn't follow suit.

- Tell your partner whether she is on the board or in her hand.

DEFENDERS
Communication between defenders can be done legally

Be extra careful when you're a defender. You don't want to lead out of turn or revoke, even if you catch it quickly. Because any mistake on your part gives information to your partner, defenders will get penalized by either one of those. Go slowly and make sure you're playing the right card.

Defenders are also in the tricky spot of possibly communicating with their partner through body language. This is a big no-no. In the top events at big tournaments, they have screens that keep the players from transmitting any unintended information. Players can only see the cards on the table and not their partners or the opponents.

Card communication, on the other hand, is not only legal, but it's a must if you want to be successful. Signaling your partner by playing a low card or a high card is a great strategy and part

Leading

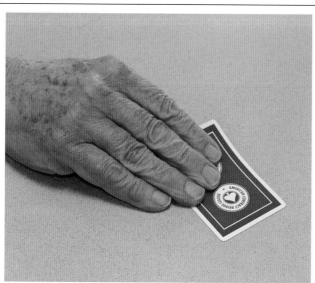

- If you think you're on lead, pull the card you plan to lead and place it facedown on the table.

- You may ask the table if you're on lead.

- Once everyone agrees you're on lead, you may turn the card over.

- If you're not on lead, you can put the card back in your hand with no penalty, because no one has seen what it is.

Catching Your Mistake

- Pay careful attention to the card you're pulling.

- If you fail to follow suit or you notice that you thought you pulled one card, but there's actually a different card on the table, say "Stop!" immediately.

- If the next player hasn't played a card yet, then your card will stay exposed to be played at the next legal moment, but you can correct your mistake.

of the fun of playing bridge. Realizing that you communicated successfully with your choice of cards is always a thrill.

Using your body, groaning after a bad lead, or changing your playing tempo is not. For instance, when your opponent plays a card and you, following suit, have the choice between the 4 and the 5 for example (no significant choice at all really), you can't deliberately hesitate, trying to fake out the opponent into thinking you have a missing honor.

Just remember, it's all about the cards.

ZOOM

If you lead out of turn, there are five options for your opponents. It can be overwhelming for a new player, and even expert players won't always be able to figure out the best option. If you're new to the game, the director will often help you through it.

Giving Information Away

- You never know what people will pay attention to, so be careful not to give information away for free.

- Don't pull a card out before it's your turn to play, even if you don't show it to the table.

- Don't rearrange your hand once you're out of a suit.

- Don't count with your fingers.

No Body Language

- Even if your partner doesn't lead back the suit of your extremely obvious singleton, you need to keep a poker face.

- If, instead, your eyes bug open and your jaw drops down in shock and horror, don't be surprised if the director is called and you're slapped with a penalty.

DUPLICATE ETIQUETTE

THE DECLARER
You're running the show, so set a good example

The first etiquette suggestion for the declarer is to thank her partner for the dummy she has placed on the table, even if she is looking at a hand that has only 2 points and is completely different from what she expected. "Thank you, partner" keeps things friendly.

However, other than the "thank you" part, the declarer is now off the hook in a communication or even body language

sense. Even if she sighs and rolls her eyes on every card, she's only informing (and annoying) the opponents. She can even lead from the wrong side and not get penalized (although she does have to correct her mistake), because she only gave defenders information.

Like the defenders, however, the declarer cannot use a prolonged hesitation to imply the possession of an honor card,

Be Polite

- When the hand comes down, be sure to thank your partner.

- Not only does this ensure goodwill at the table, but it also has a strategic component.

- If you seem frustrated or horrified by your partner's bid, then you give a clue to the opponents that you might be in a tricky contract.

Take a Minute

- Always take a minute or two to plan your strategy.

- This is much easier to do with all 26 of your cards visible, than halfway through, when a lot of them are gone and you have to rely on your memory.

- Even if there's a singleton in the suit that's led, still take the time to plan how you're going to play the rest of it.

but she may use the cards to try to fool the opponents.

For instance, many players use a "false card" when the opponents have found a good lead. They might drop a jack or a queen on the first trick, hoping that the opponent will think it's a singleton. This is using the cards to bluff and is perfectly acceptable. But don't get too hung up on trying to figure out tricky false carding plays. Your job as the declarer is to analyze the two hands before you and try to make as many tricks as possible. Take your time and get it right.

Wrong Side

- Sometimes the declarer will pull a card from her hand when she's actually in the dummy (or vice versa).

- If the next player plays, the game proceeds. If, however, the opponents or the dummy catches it, then the declarer may put her card back in her hand with no penalty.

- She then starts in the proper place.

Claiming

- If it's obvious that you have the rest of the tricks, you may claim them in order to save time.

- You don't have to play out the whole hand.

- Don't claim if you still haven't pulled all the trump. You may get penalized, even if you have higher trump.

AFTER THE HAND
There are etiquette issues even when the hand is over

Believe it or not, you still have to watch your behavior even when the hand is finished. You have to be pleasant to your partner, considerate of the opponents, and aware of the needs of the rest of the room.

No matter the magnitude of the disaster, don't blame your partner. He did the best job he could bidding and playing the hand. No one enters the game trying to play poorly. If

you have a question about why he bid or played something, write it down and revisit it later. If you have time at the end of the round, you may even be able to look at the cards.

By the same token, be kind to your opponents. Don't point out the flaws in their play. Ignorance can sometimes be bliss. If they open the traveler (score sheets that travel with the boards) and see that everyone else in the room made one

Agreement at the End

- At the end of the hand, you'll all have 13 cards laid out in some manner in front of you.

- More often than not, the cards will be lined up identically, but every so often there will be a discrepancy.

- Make sure you're all in agreement before you scoop up your cards, because you may need to reconstruct the hand.

An Interesting Hand

- Bridge fans can't help chatting about a hand, but you have to restrain yourself.

- Play all the hands at the table first.

- If you have some time once all the hands are done in that round, you can go back and revisit the tricky hand. Just make sure you do it quietly.

more trick than they did, and they ask you, then you might say something. But otherwise keep quiet.

No one should be discussing the hand until the round is over, because it can really slow up the play for everyone else. Even when the round is over, you have to be careful about your discussion. Remember that players right near you will be playing the hand next. It's not fair to anyone if someone overhears, "Wow! That makes a small slam!"

Only North Scores

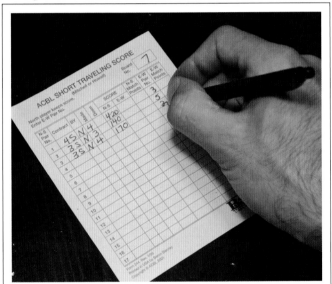

- At the end of the hand, the north player will score the game and show the score to the rest of the table for verification.

- When travelers (score sheets that travel with the boards) are used, players are often dying to know what the other tables have bid.

- If you're not north—the only player allowed to touch the traveler—resist the temptation to take a peak. You'll see it soon enough.

Always Be Nice

- Good sportsmanship and gracious behavior are always important, but because bridge is a partnership game, it's especially key to be thoughtful and considerate with your partner.

- Remember, nobody chooses to a make a mistake.

- While bridge may be the greatest game in the world, remember that it is still just a game.

OPENING BIDS SUMMARY

Opening with at least 13 points:

13–19 points:

Open on the one level.

If you have a 5-card major, bid the major.

If you have no 5-card major, bid your better minor, hoping your partner will respond with a 4-card major.

Double if the opponents have bid and you're short in their suit.

15–17 points:

With a balanced hand, bid 1NT.

Without a balanced hand, see above. If you have six cards, jump in your suit on your next bid to show points. Or if you find a fit with your partner, jump in that suit.

18–19 points:

No matter what your shape is, start the bidding on the one level and jump into a different suit or NT on your second bid (called a "jump shift").

If the opponents have already bid, double, then bid, regardless of your shape.

20–21 points:

With a balanced hand, bid 2NT.

With a long suit, count your length to get you to 2 ♣ (see below).

If the opponents have already bid, double, then bid, regardless of your shape.

2+ points:
Start with 2 clubs. This says nothing about your clubs, but it tells your partner that you have 22 or more points.
If your opponents have already bid, double, then bid, regardless of your shape.

Opening with fewer than 13 points:
6–10 high card points and a long suit (preemptive bidding).

If you have 6 of a suit (except clubs), bid 2 of that suit.
If you have 7 of a suit, bid 3 of that suit.

Unless your partner bids NT or a new suit (both forcing bids), do not bid again. You have only this one bid.

Points recommended to bid to game/slam:

3NT: 26 high card points

4 ♠ or 4 ♥: 26 points, can be from distribution

5 ♦ or 5 ♣: 29 points, can be from distribution

6 of anything (small slam): 33 points (including distribution if you're in a suit)

7 of anything (grand slam): 37 points (including distribution if you're in a suit)

RESPONDING BIDS SUMMARY

Response to a suit bid:

0–5 points:

>Pass.

6–9 points:

>Support your partner's suit on the two level.
>
>Bid on the one level (new suit or 1NT).

10–12 points:

>Support your partner's suit on the three level.
>
>Introduce a new suit on the one or two level.

13+ points:

>With support for your partner's suit, first bid a new suit. Then jump to game.

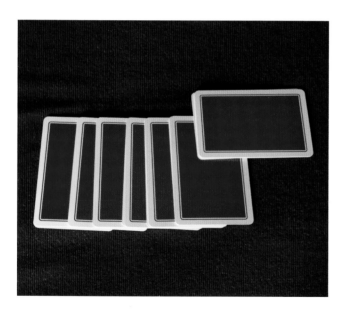

Without support, make sure you make forcing bids until you get to game. Pay attention to your partner's bidding to see if you have the points for slam, and make sure you don't close out in game if you do.

Response to a 1NT bid:

0–7 points:

>With a five(+)-card major, bid 2 ♦ or 2 ♥ to transfer. Do not bid again.
>
>Without a 5-card major, pass.

8–9 points:

>With a five(+)-card major, transfer, then invite to game.
>
>With a 4-card major, use Stayman, then invite to game.
>
>With neither, bid 2NT (invitational).

10+ points:

      With a five(+)-card major, transfer, then force to game.

      With a 4-card major, use Stayman, then force to game.

      With neither, bid 3NT.

Response to a preemptive bid:

0–13 points:

      Continue the preempt if you're not vulnerable.

14+ points:

      If you have a fit, jump to game or look for slam.

      If you don't have a fit, and NT seems like a possibility, bid 2NT (feature asking).

      If you have a long suit of your own, bid it (forcing one round).

DUPLICATE SCORING SUMMARY

Tricks

30 points per trick for majors
20 points per trick for minors
40 points for first trick in NT, 30 for subsequent tricks

Bonus points

50 points for a partial game bid
300 points for a nonvulnerable game
500 points for a vulnerable game

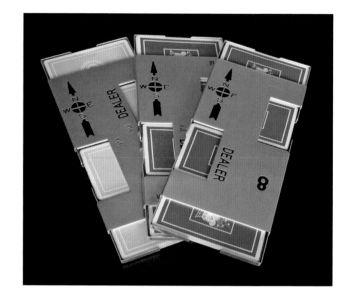

Defensive points

50 points per trick for defenders when nonvulnerable contract is set
100 points per trick for defenders when vulnerable contract is set

Doubled but not vulnerable per trick: 100, 300, 500, 800
Doubled and vulnerable per trick: 200, 500, 800, 1,100

Adding it up

If you make your bid, you get the points. If you don't, the defense gets the points—50 or 100 points (depending on vulnerability) for each trick that you said you would get but didn't.

If you do make your bid, count the number of tricks you bid and multiply by the appropriate major/minor number. If that number is under 100, you did not make game, but you get a 50-point bonus for making your bid. Then add any overtricks you might have. Vulnerability does not come into play.

If you reach 100 points or higher, you've made game. If you make game you get a game bonus: 300 or 500 depending on vulnerability. Then add the overtricks.

ACBL SHORT TRAVELING SCORE
(Mitchell or Howell)

North player keeps score.
Enter E-W Pair No.

Board No. 7

N-S Pair No.	Contract	BY	Made	Down	SCORE N-S	SCORE E-W	N-S Match Points	E-W Pair No.	E-W Match Points
1	4 S	N	4		420			3	
2	3 S	N	3		140			5	
3	3 S	N	4		170			2	
4	3 S	N	5		200			4	
5									
6									
7									
8									
9									
10									

ACBL

The following information was taken from the American Contract Bridge League (ACBL) Web site: www.ACBL.org

The American Contract Bridge League is the governing body for duplicate bridge in North America. It is the largest bridge organization in the world, with more than 160,000 members living in the United States, Canada, Mexico, and Bermuda. A not-for-profit organization, the ACBL determines internationally recognized rules of bridge, sanctions clubs and tournament games, and encourages participation at all levels of proficiency and experience.

Founded: 1937
Headquarters: Memphis, Tennessee
Annual dues: $35 ($26 for first-year members)
Annual budget: $18 million

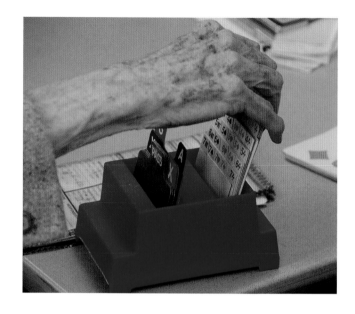

The ACBL supports:

• 3 million tables of bridge in play annually in clubs and tournaments and an additional 300,000 tables online

• 3,200 bridge clubs

• 1,100 bridge tournaments annually

The ACBL certifies:

• Bridge directors and teachers

• Player achievement through masterpoints

The ACBL sponsors:

- Three North American Bridge Championships annually, each attracting up to 8,000 players

- The School Bridge Lesson Series Program for more than 4,000 children annually

Publications:

- *The Bridge Bulletin* magazine, the world's most popular bridge publication

- *The ACBL Bridge Series* for bridge instruction

- *Learn to Play Bridge* (Free Software)

- *Laws of Duplicate Bridge*

- *Laws of Contract Bridge*

MASTERPOINT MILESTONES

The following table comes from the ACBL Web site at www.ACBL.org. Note that the requirements for Life Master will be modified as of January 1, 2010. Anyone who is a registered member of the ACBL before that date will be allowed to gain Life Master status under the old qualifications.

Title	Masterpoints Earned
Rookie	Fewer than 5
Junior Master	5
Club Master	20
Sectional Master	50 (5 must be silver)
Regional Master	100 (15 silver, 5 red or gold)
NABC Master	200 (50 pigmented, with at least 5 gold, 15 red or gold, and 25 silver) 300 (50 silver, 25 gold, and 25 red or gold)
Life Master	As of January 1, 2010, the requirements for attaining Life Master status will change to 500 total masterpoints, of which 50 must be gold or platinum; 50 red, gold, or platinum; 75 silver; and 75 black.
Bronze Life Master	500
Silver Life Master	1,000
Gold Life Master	2,500
Diamond Life Master	5,000
Emerald Life Master	7,500
Platinum Life Master	10,000
Grand Life Master	10,000 and see below*

*This is the highest rank in the ACBL. It requires 10,000 masterpoints and one victory in a North American Bridge Championship with no upper masterpoint restriction or an Open Team Trials or its equivalent or a Women's Team Trials or its equivalent or any of the following WBF events: Bermuda Bowl, Venice Cup, Rosenblum Cup, McConnell Cup, Open Pairs, Women's Pairs, Olympiad, Women's Team Olympiad, WBF Senior Pairs event, WBF World Swiss Teams, WBF World Mixed Teams, and WBF Senior Teams.

237

GLOSSARY

Auction: the process of determining the trump suit

Balanced Hand: a hand usually defined by no voids, no singletons, and no more than one doubleton

Balancing Seat: the player whose pass would end the auction

Bidding Box: a device used by duplicate bridge players to make the bid visually rather than orally

Blackwood: an ace-asking convention

Book: the first 6 tricks earned by the declarer

Breaking a Suit: leading a suit for the first time

Broken Strength: (also called a tenace) two nontouching honors, missing the honor in between

Cappalletti: a convention for interfering over no trump

Chicago Scoring: a method of scoring that mimics duplicate scoring when there are only four players

Contract: the result of the auction

Convenient Minor: a convention that uses the minors to get to the majors

Cue Bid: bidding a suit artificially to convey information

Danger Suit: a suit (especially in no trump contracts) that the declarer wants to avoid

Declarer: the player who declared the trump suit first in the pair who won the auction

Defenders: the pair that did not win the auction

Director: a certified supervisor for a duplicate game

Discard: the card played when a player cannot follow suit and does not play trump

Double Fit: when the partnership has at least 8 cards in each of two suits

Doubleton: only 2 cards in a suit

Dummy: the partner of the declarer and the player who displays the hand on the table

Duplicate Bridge: a method of bridge competition where players all play the same hands

Feature: usually an ace or a protected king

Finesse: a gamble when a player is missing an honor

Fit: an 8-card combination in a partnership

Following Suit: playing a card from the same suit as the card that was led

Game: 100 points and the most likely goal of the bidders during the auction

Gerber: an ace-asking convention

Grand Slam: bidding and taking all 13 tricks

High Card Points: the points a player uses to evaluate the strength of his hand

Honor Cards: ace, king, queen, jack, and ten

Jump Shift: when a player changes suits and goes up a level higher than he needs to

Lead: the first card in a trick

Major Suits: spades and hearts

Matchpoints: the method of scoring to evaluate the various tables' performances at duplicate

Michaels: a convention used to describe a two-suited hand

Minor Suits: clubs and diamonds

Negative Double: a convention used in response to show four of the other major

No Trump: one of the bidding choices in the auction that results in no trump suit for the hand

Opening: being the first player to bid in the auction

Overcall: the second player to bid in the auction

Overtrick: any tricks over the stated number of tricks from the auction

Penalty Double: a bid that forces the number of points—on either side—to be increased

Pulling Trump: getting rid of the opponents' trump cards

Quantitative Bidding: asking a partner to clarify if he's at the low end or high end of his bid

Raise: rebidding a partner's suit at a higher level

Redouble: a bid that may only be used after a double and if left in increases the points even more

Responder: the partner of the opener

Roman Key Card: an ace-asking convention

Rubber Bridge: a method of scoring for four people

Sequence: touching cards, usually honors

Set: when a partnership does not achieve the stated contract

Side Suit: a long suit that is not the trump suit

Singleton: only 1 card in a suit

Small Slam: bidding and taking 12 of 13 tricks

Stayman: a response to no trump that promises at least one 4-card major

Stopper: a card that will keep the opponents from running a long suit in no trump

Takeout Double: an artificial use of the double bid to ask a partner to bid anything but the opponent's suit

Tally: a card to record the scores for party bridge

Transfer: an artificial bid after no trump to allow the stronger hand to bid the suit

Trick: 4 cards, one from each player

Trump: the all-powerful suit that was decided during the auction

Underleading: leading a low card in a suit that has an honor

Unusual No Trump: a convention that describes two 5-card suits

Void: no cards in a suit

Vulnerability: a designation that raises the point level for the vulnerable partnership. Happens after winning a game in rubber bridge or on a rotational basis in duplicate bridge

Weak Two Bid: a preemptive bid that shows 6 cards in a suit but few high card points

INDEX